Road to Rescue
Dog Rescue Best Practices Manual

Written by Kyla Duffy

Edited by Susan Tauber

Published by Up For Pups

Road to Rescue, a best practices manual published to improve the effectiveness and sustainability of dog rescue organizations, was created with the help of numerous principled, experienced rescuers.

Up For Pups is a small 501(c)3 humane education organization that relies exclusively on donations to continue providing valuable resources for rescuers, such as this manual. If this manual has helped your organization, please consider making a donation by mailing a check to Up For Pups, 3110 Gatling Lane, Boulder, CO 80301 or clicking the "donate" link at http://upforpups.org/.

Road to Rescue Best Practices Manual by Up For Pups

Written by Kyla Duffy

Edited by Susan Tauber

Published by Up For Pups, www.upforpups.org

The publisher gratefully acknowledges the rescuers who participated in the creation of this book and who generously offer their time and skills to save dogs in need.

Any brand names mentioned in this book are registered trademarks and the property of their owners. The author and publishing company make no claims to them.

Photo Credits:

Cover image: Jaime Rowe, http://jaimerowephotography.com

Publishers Cataloging In Publication Available Upon Request

ISBN (paperback): 978-0-9833126-3-5

Acknowledgements

Up For Pups is grateful to the following upstanding private rescue organizations for their assistance in the development of this manual:

- Adopt a Rescued Friend
- Alliston & District Humane Society
- Arizona Golden Retriever Connection
- DARE
- Dogs 2nd Chance
- Golden Retriever Freedom Rescue
- GRRAND
- Houston Beagle and Hound Rescue
- It's the Pits
- Legacy Boxer Rescue
- MidAmerica Boston Terrier Rescue
- Mile High Weimaraner Rescue
- Nebraska Border Collie Rescue
- Northern Chesapeake Sheltie Rescue
- Pug Partners of Nebraska
- Small Dog Rescue of Minnesota

Up For Pups would like to extend a special thanks to Jennifer Misfeldt of MidAmerica Boston Terrier Rescue, Lorie Huston of the Pet Health Care Gazette, Sharon Sleighter of Legacy Boxer Rescue, and Shereen Raucci of Mile High Weimaraner Rescue for their unwavering support and thoughtful participation in the creation of this manual. We would also like to thank Susan Tauber for her positive attitude, dedication to our mission, and willingness to give her best effort, no matter what.

A Note to Rescuers

Dear Rescuers,

Dog rescue is about <u>saving lives.</u> It is *not* about money, egos, territorial claims, or social status. While this fact may seem obvious, the dog rescue industry, since its inception, has been plagued by organizations working against each other instead of with each other. This negative behavior is counterproductive to any reputable organization's stated mission. Nevertheless, change can start with *you.*

The creation of this manual is a step in the right direction. We are grateful to the rescuers who generously shared their experiences throughout the manual's development process, and we hope the rescue industry continues to move in this positive, collaborative direction.

We also wish to remind you that rescue organizations primarily exist to <u>facilitate</u> adoptions. The Latin word for "easy" is facilis, which helps to remind us that "facilitate" means to make something easy. That is not to say that a dog should be allowed to walk away with anyone who is interested, but it does mean giving animal-loving people who can provide a safe environment for a pet a fair chance to adopt a dog of their choice. It means evaluating each dog and each adopter as individuals and recognizing that what is not safe for one animal may be safe for another. (E.g., some dogs need six-foot-high fences whereas others can be walked easily on a leash.) It means giving timely feedback to potential adopters who don't meet your rescue's adoption standards, so the applicants can change their situation, if possible, to become qualified applicants. And it means helping move dogs into an adoptable state to the best of your rescue's ability by treating injuries, illnesses, and behavioral issues; by grooming them; and by advertising them with honest descriptions in places where potential adopters are likely to find them (online, local newspapers, adoption events, etc.).

For experienced rescuers reading this manual, we hope you'll take these words to heart and use this book as an opportunity to reevaluate yourself and your organization, using your discoveries as a basis to answer the question, "What more can my organization do on its own and in collaboration with others to save the most lives?" For new rescuers, this manual will be an indispensible road map on your path to success.

Up For Pups will continuously update *Road to Rescue* as we receive new ideas and information. We welcome your comments and questions. You can provide feedback directly on each topic by following the "Rescuers Ring In" link at the end of each chapter, or you can reach us through http://upforpups.org/contact.

For the dogs,

Kyla Duffy

Director, Up For Pups

Table of Contents

Introduction and Definitions

The nation's largest pet adoption database, Petfinder.com, showcases well over 10,000 "adoption groups" listing hundreds of thousands of adoptable animals at any given time. Many of these groups are private animal rescue organizations that are operated out of people's homes, with a network of transport and foster volunteers who support the immense number of animals these rescues save each year. Despite the fact that this industry is obviously sizable and growing, it is virtually unregulated without even a best practices handbook for rescues to use as a reference.*

To create this manual, Up For Pups collaborated with numerous experienced, diverse private rescue organizations and animal welfare societies. After developing the project outline, each rescue wrote about two or three topics, which were subsequently posted on the Up For Pups blog for public discussion. The beginning of the discussion can be found at http://upforpups.org/2011/02/best-practices-manual/. The entire data-collection and editing period spanned six months, and Up For Pups continues to monitor comments on these blog posts for information to add to this manual.

The purpose of this manual is to

- Help new rescues "do it right" from the beginning.

- Give existing rescues a "measuring stick" and guide for maximum effectiveness.

- Present a foundation for evaluating rescue effectiveness for those interested in donating and providing grants.

Careful observation of the practices outlined in this manual will help rescues save the most lives, spend the least money, and ensure a good experience for both volunteers and rescued animals. Up For

---

* Manuals and standards are available for shelters, but "rescues" generally run very differently from shelters and cannot necessarily follow similar practices.

Pups recognizes that dog rescue is not a one-size-fits-all effort and that some upstanding rescues may have policies that differ from those listed herein, but regardless of size or breed, some practices are better than others, which is what we've set out to highlight.

Book Organization

Several rescues have been kind enough to provide us with examples of their contracts and documents to give you a foundation for creating your own documents. The Appendix symbol is used throughout the book to indicate when we have included examples of documents in *Appendix A*. We ask that you use these examples as learning tools only. Using them verbatim is plagiarism, and you'll need to adapt them for your rescue's use anyway.

Appendix B is available only to people who have purchased the paperback copy of the book (that means you!). It includes documents that have been created specifically for rescue use. They are provided in .doc format, so as to be easy to edit as necessary.

Underlined text indicates hyperlinks to websites and references to other chapters. Check the "Resources" section at the end of each chapter for links associated with the underlined words. The "Resources" section additionally includes a hyperlink called "Rescuers Ring In." This link points to the first post in the initial blog discussion that served as the foundation for each chapter. Follow these links to see what experienced rescuers have to say about each topic.

The last page of each chapter also includes the following helpful symbols to identify issues of particular importance:

 Ideas and practices *to follow.*

 Ideas and practices *to avoid.*

Disclaimer

Road to Rescue focuses on decentralized dog rescue organizations that function primarily through foster homes. Up For Pups is considering subsequent manuals for other types of organizations, like cat rescues, mixed-species rescues, and centralized rescues with common facilities housing their adoptable animals.

Road to Rescue *is not exhaustive. Rescuers will encounter situations not outlined in this manual and will need to treat specific situations differently than discussed herein. Rescuers should consult professionals for their specific needs, especially for legal and financial items.*

Definitions

Breeder: A person who mates dogs. Animal welfare organizations generally refer to several different kinds of breeders. Note that the AKC (American Kennel Club) may provide certification to *any* of the following, so AKC certification is not necessarily an indication of good breeding practices:

Backyard breeder: A person or family that breeds dogs without comprehensive knowledge of breeding. Sometimes people breed dogs to "show children the miracle of life," while other times people do it to make money. For whatever reason, the resulting puppies, be they mutts or purebred, generally are not of particular good breed stock and tend to have a high incidence of undesirable physical and psychological characteristics.

Commercial breeder (puppy mill): One who usually breeds multiple breeds of dogs and has profit as the primary motive for existence. Canine health and environmental cleanliness vary among facilities but are known for being substandard. The dogs usually are not screened for genetic diseases, and the breeding stock is generally not carefully selected for resemblance to the breed standard or for good temperament. Most commercial breeders sell their puppies to pet stores or to brokers, who then resell them to pet stores. Many puppy mills have hundreds or thousands of breeding dogs at a time.

Reputable breeder: A breed fancier who usually has only one breed (but may have more); follows a breeding plan in effort to preserve and protect the breed; produces only a few litters per year; breeds only when a litter will enhance the breed and the breeding program; raises the puppies with plenty of environmental and human contact; has a contract that protects the breeder, dog, and buyer, including a clause about taking the dog back for any reason; runs a small, clean kennel; screens breeding stock to reduce hereditary defects from the breed; works with a breed club or kennel club to promote and protect the breed; supports the work of rescue organizations; and cares that each and every puppy is placed in the best home possible.

Breed club: Breed clubs are organizations formed by fanciers around a specific breed of animal. Breed clubs engage in many breed-related activities including defining breed standards, compiling a list of breeders and rescues, and hosting breed-related events. The clubs may or may not be associated with the American Kennel Club (AKC) or other national organizations. Some breed clubs have volunteers engaged in rescue under the management of the club itself.

Distributors:

Broker: An organization (or person) that buys puppies from commercial kennels and sells them to retail outlets. Brokers ship puppies throughout the country by the crate-full using planes and trucks. Brokers must be licensed by the United States Department of Agriculture (USDA) and must abide by the shipping regulations in its Animal Welfare Act.

Buncher: An organization (or person) that collects dogs of unknown origin for sale to laboratories or other bunchers and brokers. Bunchers are suspected of buying stolen pets, of collecting pets advertised as "free to a good home," and of adopting unwanted pets from animal shelters and then selling them to institutions that use dogs for research.

<u>Guardian:</u> A term often preferred by rescues when referring to the primary caretaker of a dog. The difficulty with this term is that it has certain legal implications that do not actually apply to the relationship between caretaker and canine. Nevertheless, many feel that the term "guardian" is better than "owner" because it implies that a dog is more than just a thing people "own."

Independent rescuer: An individual who plays a role in the care and re-homing of needy animals but is not officially associated with an incorporated rescue organization.

Owner: While the terms "guardian" and "owner" are used somewhat interchangeably throughout this manual, "owner" generally refers to a person who has a dog but does not provide the proper care to him or her.

Rescue: For the purpose of this manual, the term "rescue," when used as a noun, refers to decentralized dog rescue organizations – organizations housing displaced dogs in foster homes as opposed to a central shelter – which is supported by charitable contributions. When used as a verb, the term relates to the act of taking a dog into a rescue organization.

Forever home: A term used to describe an adoptive family.

Foster: This term is used for several ideas associated with temporarily housing an animal in a home. A *foster* home is a home that provides a safe environment for an animal until a suitable adoptive family can be found. A *foster* dog is a dog currently housed in a foster home. A *foster* parent is the person charged with caring for a foster dog. *Fostering* is the act of caring for animas in one's home until they are placed in forever homes.

Re-home: To take dogs from one situation and find them a new, more suitable, permanent home.

Shelter: An establishment, usually supported by charitable contributions and/or municipal funding, which provides a temporary home for dogs, cats, and other displaced animals. Examples of shelters are local humane societies and facilities associated with the American Society for the Prevention of Cruelty to Animals (ASPCA). Shelters are also sometimes referred to as "pounds," specifically when the shelter has a relationship with the local animal control office.

Shelter/rescue categorizations: Shelters and rescues are sometimes identified using the following terms:

o **Kill:** This term is used to describe shelters and rescues that euthanize animals for a variety of reasons:

- Illness (major or minor)

- Disabilities

- Age (too young or too old to re-home)

- Temperament (treatable or untreatable issues)

- Overcrowding

- Breed

o **No-kill:** A no-kill shelter or rescue does not euthanize animals for population control and only euthanizes animals if they are too sick to be treated or too aggressive for adoption.[i] However, the definitions of "incurable" illness or aggression are sometimes defined to fit individual organizations' agendas. There are very few shelters in the country that truly uphold no-kill standards as they are meant to be.

o **Limited admission:** A shelter or rescue that turns away animals that do not fit its parameters (e.g., a dog is too old, too sick, or the "wrong" breed).

o **Open admission:** A shelter or rescue that takes in any animal it receives.

Spay/neuter: The removal of an animal's reproductive organs. This procedure is recommended for population control and for the health and safety of the pet, unless the animal has a preexisting medical condition wherein anesthesia would put him or her at an unreasonable risk of death. If performed at a young age, this procedure helps reduce the occurrence of certain maladies and aggressive behavior.

Other Vocabulary Notes

In this manual, you'll notice that dogs are always referred to as "he" or "she," as opposed to "it." Dogs obviously have gender, thoughts, and feelings. Referring to dogs as "who" instead of "what" is not only appropriate, but it reinforces the idea that dogs are not just "things."

The *Road to Rescue* is written using terms that reinforce a mutual respect between dog and guardian. When talking with people about their pets, you can carefully choose your words to do the same. For example, "house training" is a much more positive term than "house breaking," which to some may imply that harsh methods must be used. Word choice may seem simple, but it can completely change the way people think about their relationships with their dogs.

Chapter 1:
A Brief History of Dog Rescue Organizations

The animal welfare movement is well-documented in books and on websites. Even so, pinpointing the impetus for the growth of *private dog rescue organizations* is difficult for several reasons:

- Rescues are generally private entities requiring limited recordkeeping.

- Most non-profit animal welfare organizations do not have time or money for comprehensive archiving.

- There is no one entity governing private rescue organizations or recording their activities.

Despite a lack of documentation, by studying the development of animal welfare organizations throughout history, we can draw several conclusions about the origins of private rescues:

Animal Exploitation

At least some private rescue organizations were formed in response to post-World War II trends that caused the increased exploitation of animals. For example, some of the first documented private animal rescue organizations were for Greyhounds. Greyhound racing started in 1912, when the mechanical lure was invented. The first circular track opened in 1919.[ii] The sport was most popular after WWII but experienced a decline after the 1960 Betting and Gaming Act permitted off-course cash betting. The sport again soared in popularity in the 1980s, at which time many press articles about Greyhounds emphasized that they were unsuitable as family pets by showing pictures of them wearing muzzles and describing them as bloodthirsty killers.

Before Greyhound rescues existed, these dogs almost invariably faced euthanization at the end of their careers. In the United States, the first documented rescue organization was founded in 1974, when a

Connecticut woman named Eileen McCaughern adopted a Greyhound, a practice that was practically unheard of at the time. From there she began rescuing and re-homing Greyhounds. McCaughern still operates today as <u>Retired Greyhounds as Pets of CT</u>, which for a brief time was a faction of the larger Retried Greyhounds as Pets (REGAP) organization started in Florida in 1982 by Ron Walsek. The founding of this organization is said to be the true beginning of the Greyhound rescue movement, and by 1986, REGAP had representatives in many East Coast states. With the exception of some of the founding members, who chose to remain independent, these representatives came together to form <u>Greyhound Pets of America (GPA)</u>, which still operates all over the country today, in addition to many other independent Greyhound rescue organizations.[iii] At the time of publication, the Internal Revenue Service database had 214 rescues organizations with the word "Greyhound" listed in their names.

The rise of puppy mills, a significant setback in animal welfare after WWII, may be equal to Greyhound racing as a catalyst for the relatively recent proliferation of private rescue organizations and their tendency to focus specifically on taking in abused dogs and finding them good homes. Puppy mills began as a result of a drought following WWII, at which time Midwestern farmers seeking alternative sources of income started filling their rabbit hutches with dogs, breeding them cycle after cycle, and selling them to retail pet stores.[iv] While farmers saw big profits, animal welfare advocates saw suffering dogs creating sick puppies and took measures to help these animals by starting rescues to get these dogs out of their deplorable living conditions.

Fragmentation of Animal Welfare Organizations

A variety of animal welfare organizations evolved throughout the decades alongside socioeconomic change, so the growth of private animal rescue organizations was inevitable. When progress was made on one issue, the organizations moved on to other issues. Some organizations used shock tactics, which have been successful in garnering media attention for causes, but these tactics have also resulted in divisions between more- and less-radical members.

Additionally, the animal welfare movement has always suffered from internal disagreements, thus causing organizational fractures, which have often resulted in new organizations that are more or less radical than previous organizations.

One conservative strategy adopted by some organizations is the practice of working together *with* the people and/or groups that are treating animals cruelly, in order to foster positive change. This approach is a component of many animal rescue organizations, as many work with puppy mills, laboratories that test on animals, backyard breeders, etc. to get dogs out of those situations and on the road to good homes.

Breed Clubs

Some rescue organizations were born from breed clubs (see *Introduction and Definitions*). Some breed clubs have a rescue branch while others skirt the idea of rescue for liability or other reasons, which has caused rescue-oriented club members to start their own organizations.

Filling Community Needs

While a growing number of shelters are soliciting the help of foster parents to care for animals with special needs until they are ready for adoption, some shelter adopters and volunteers have seen a greater need for foster homes than the shelters provide and therefore have decided to start their own rescue organizations.

Women in Rescue

Historically, women were not able to take leadership roles in animal welfare organizations until after the end of WWII (1945), but the presence of women in prominent roles did much to shape the ideology of the movement thereafter.[v] This fact becomes obvious when one takes a roll call of private dog rescue organizations today. The majority are run by women. In 1870, Caroline Earle White secured funding and municipal support for the nation's first public animal shelter in Philadelphia, which was the beginning of a national trend.[vi]

In summary, the ASPCA organization that defined animal welfare in the United States, was formed by Henry Bergh in April 1866.[vii] As of 2006, there were more than 7,000 organizations, representing over 10 million members, dedicated to animal welfare issues.[viii] Sadly, this growth points to an increased need for champions of animal welfare, but it also indicates that many have risen to answer the call.

Resources

Rescuers Ring In:
http://upforpups.org/2011/02/best-practices-the-history-of-rescue/

Animal rights history from antiquity through the early 20th century:
http://www.animalrightshistory.org/

Beers, Diane L. 2006. For the Prevention of Cruelty: *The History and Legacy of Animal Rights Activism in the United States.* Swallow Press.

Greyhound Pets of America: http://www.greyhoundpets.org/

Retired Greyhounds as Pets: http://www.regapct.com/

Works Cited:

i.   http://en.wikipedia.org/wiki/No-kill_shelter

ii.   http://en.wikipedia.org/wiki/Greyhound_racing#History

iii. Dillon, Joan. Greyhound Adoption Pioneers. http://s335837781.onlinehome.us/pdfs/Greyhound%20Adoption%20Pioneers.pdf

iv.   http://www.prisonersofgreed.org/USDA.html

v.   Beers, Diane L. 2006. For the Prevention of Cruelty to Animals. Swallow Press, Ohio. P3.

vi.   Beers, Diane L. 2006. For the Prevention of Cruelty to Animals. Swallow Press, Ohio. P73.

vii.   Beers, Diane L. 2006. For the Prevention of Cruelty to Animals. Swallow Press, Ohio. P3.

viii.   National Anti-Vivisection Society. 1994. In Defense of the Defenseless. *Expressions 2.* 28.

Chapter 2:
Rescues and Shelters

Both rescues and shelters have an interest and an important role in animal welfare; however, they generally operate very differently.

Most **rescues** are decentralized in that they don't have a central facility. They usually operate out of people's homes, utilizing a network of volunteers to rescue and re-home animals. Usually rescues do not have paid positions. They are either founded and run by one individual or they are governed by a board, with board members eligible for reelection or rotated out at intervals stated in the rescue organization bylaws. Either way, the positions are generally voluntary and result in no monetary compensation. Some rescues are breed-specific or oriented around a certain "type" of animal (e.g., Pug rescue, dog rescue, cat rescue, horse rescue, puppy mill rescue, vivisection rescue, etc.), while others take in any needy animals. Veterinary care for animals "saved" by rescue organizations is usually provided by local veterinarians at a discounted fee. Rescues typically have extensive adoption processes including applications, home checks, and reference checks. Funding for rescues is most often obtained through private donors, grants, and fundraising events.

Shelters generally house animals in a centralized location with minimal use of foster homes only for desperate cases. They usually utilize a combination of paid staff members and volunteers to care for these animals and are often city-run or city-sponsored. The types of animals that shelters take in varies from shelter to shelter, with some taking only dogs and cats and others including reptiles, rodents, birds, and sometimes even wildlife. Some shelters have onsite veterinary clinics, while others either don't provide veterinary care or provide it through offsite veterinarians. The shelter adoption process is usually much less stringent than the rescue adoption process: a potential adopter meets dogs, fills out an application, and goes home with a dog on the same day.

Although both rescues and shelters can either be no-kill, high-kill, or somewhere in-between (see the *Introduction and Definitions* section for definitions), reputable rescues only euthanize the animals in their care who have incurable, painful diseases or show dangerous and unmanageable aggression, which is discussed in detail in <u>*Chapter 5: Legal Concerns.*</u> Admission to a rescue depends on the rescue's mission, be it a purebred rescue, small dog rescue, or rescue of dogs in general, but most rescues do all they can to take in dogs regardless of medical history. Taking in dogs with serious behavioral issues is generally a much more difficult decision than taking in dogs with medical issues because while most rescues have access to veterinary care, they often do not have the resources necessary to rehabilitate dogs who are truly a danger to society.

Relationship between Shelters and Rescues

There is a continuing need for shelters and rescues to work together to save animals. Some shelters have relationships with local rescue organizations, which they call upon when they receive an animal that fits a specific rescue's "type." This relationship helps the shelters thin out their "inventory" and ensures more personalized care for dogs who are scared, ill, old, or "less adoptable" due to behavioral reasons. By working with rescues, shelters can decrease their euthanization rates.

Shelters are not obligated to work with rescues, so a mutual respect must be maintained between rescues and shelters to develop a relationship that facilitates the saving of lives. One way to ensure a good relationship with shelters is to encourage specific volunteers to learn all they can about local shelters and to walk through them weekly or monthly, offering to pull (take) dogs who fit the rescue's mission. Most shelters require rescues to be 501(c)3 non-profit entities in order to pull dogs, though some unincorporated rescuers partner with federally registered non-profit rescues to help dogs. However, many rescue organizations feel uncomfortable pulling dogs for unassociated rescuers because of liability reasons.

The degree that shelters and rescues work together is highly variable. Some shelters regularly utilize and clearly appreciate their rescue partners, whereas others almost seem to step in the way of rescues that want to help dogs. The important thing to remember is that, for the most part, people get involved in animal welfare because they love animals, or at the very least, they believe it is their moral duty to protect animals. There have been many blog posts and news articles attacking employees of shelters with high euthanasia rates, but this attitude is completely unproductive and unfair. Shelters provide entire communities with services related to animal welfare. This is no small task, and their efforts, in most cases, are genuine. The employees of shelters and volunteers of rescues both have it in their hearts to save animals, so the best thing for everyone is to **find ways to work together.** *Strong* and *constant* communication and cooperation is vital to successful shelter relationships.

Note that some states require you to license your rescue to be able to operate and to pull dogs from shelters. Check with your state animal inspectors to find out the requirements for the states in which you operate. Note that rescues covering multiple states may need multiple licenses.

> "LBR (Legacy Boxer Rescue) printed magnets for our shelters. Each magnet has pictures to represent the boxer breed, featuring a fawn, brindle-and-white version of the breed. It states, "Got BOXERS?" and lists our contact information including our toll free number and intake email address. Just another way to help make sure that BIN's (Boxer In Need) don't fall through cracks in a system full of nooks, cracks, and crannies." *–Sharon Sleighter, Legacy Boxer Rescue, TX*

Relationship between Rescues and Local Law Enforcement

Rescues may or may not interact with local law enforcement. For rescues that do work with law enforcement agencies, keeping a clear head and remembering that you are both working toward a common goal ¬—animal welfare—is imperative. These governmental agencies sometimes need prodding, but if their work is hindered by a rescue's actions, it is as good as helping the perpetrator. For example, if a rescue starts pulling dogs out of a situation before law enforcement completes the appropriate investigation and paperwork, a lawsuit may become impossible, and the charges against the perpetrator may have to be dropped.

Sometimes persuading law enforcement officials to enforce animal cruelty and neglect laws can be difficult. While there are many empathetic officers in the field, there are also some who do not care about animal welfare as much as they should, so do not simply assume that law enforcement personnel will follow up on reported animal cruelty cases. While rescues are not able to *enforce* the law, there are things rescues can do. Most people are eligible to receive humane agent certification,* which allows them to investigate cases. The requirements vary from state to state and city to city. Rescues can help gather evidence to support law enforcement in doing its job, and rescues can persistently "encourage" law enforcement officials to address an issue that appears to be slipping through the cracks (keeping a log of calls, contacts, and conversations is imperative). Asking multiple people to call on one issue is always a good strategy.

Practical Advice: Working with Shelters

If your rescue is interested in working with your local shelter, the first thing to do is to contact its program director and provide your proof of 501(c)3 status. The next step is to politely discuss the shelter's procedures and ensure that they have your name and phone number on file for when they get your specific type of dog in. From there, it is important to regularly communicate with that shelter to ensure you receive information about needy animals who fit your mission.

---

* *A Google search for the term "Humane Agent" and your state is a good place to start for information about certification in your area.*

Some shelters maintain "Do Not Transfer" (DNT) lists, which list rescue organizations the shelter believes to be disreputable. You don't want to find your organization on one of these lists! If you are considering transferring one of your foster dogs to an organization that is unknown to you, you might consider checking with local shelters to ensure the organization is not on one of these lists.

Do:

- DO get to know your local animal shelter and animal control officials.

- DO find out their preferred means of communication and keep in touch regularly.

- DO follow shelter procedures for pulling dogs and ensure you have the proper licensing.

- DO treat shelter officials with respect.

- DO work within the law (not against it).

Don't:

- DON'T go outside of the shelter chain of command to pull dogs.

- DON'T take strays into your rescue without notifying local shelters and abiding by state lost-and-found rules.

Resources

Rescuers Ring In: http://upforpups.org/2011/03/best-practices-comparison-of-rescues-and-shelters/

Winograd, Nathan J. 2009. Redemption: *The Myth of Pet Overpopulation and the No-Kill Revolution in America.* Almaden Books.

Chapter 3:
Starting a Rescue

Loving dogs is not enough to run a successful rescue, and the decision to start a rescue should not be taken lightly. There are many emotional, situational, and financial considerations. Many new rescues underestimate the time, expense, and problems associated with running a rescue and soon find themselves overwhelmed and unable to do the right thing for the animals in their care. Rescue organizations must anticipate unforeseen problems like injuries, illnesses, and contagious disease and must have a plan to deal with them. There is no greater failure than becoming unable to care for the animals you "rescue" because you did not properly plan your organization. Careful planning and honest introspection can help you decide whether starting your own rescue or volunteering with an existing rescue is right for you.

"We started NBCR when we saw many Border Collies being put down simply because they were acting like Border Collies. We believed that someone familiar with the breed should be working with the dogs and finding appropriate homes for them, and we felt that the public needed to be better educated about the breed. The movie Babe caused many people to buy Border Collie puppies without a clue as to their needs. We thought our rescue could save dogs from being euthanized and also teach the new owners how to work with their dogs. –Karen Batreall, Nebraska Border Collie Rescue

Why Start a Rescue

If you're interested in starting a rescue because you just found out how many dogs are euthanized in shelters each year and you want to do something to help save them, volunteering with an existing rescue or shelter may be the best choice. On the other hand, many rescues are born out of a community need. For example, if the local shelters are inundated with black dogs and nobody is serving their needs, starting a black dog rescue might be a great idea. (Known as black dog syndrome, black dogs are often the last to get adopted out of shelters due to dim shelter lighting and/or people's superstitions.) Another reason people start rescues is because, after working with an existing rescue, they develop different ideas about how a rescue should run and decide to go for it on their own.

Look around and see what rescues already exist. Is there one that fits your interests where you can volunteer? Is there a need for the type of rescue that you are most interested in? Above all else, remember that running a rescue is hard work, and the only way to succeed is to be extremely passionate and diligent about your rescue. Do not expect to rely on volunteers to pick up all of the work because reliable volunteers are hard to find and keep. Of course, volunteers are an integral part of running a rescue, but in the beginning, you'll be doing most of the work. Volunteering with an existing rescue is a good way to find out if you have the drive and desire to start your own.

Personal Considerations

Starting a rescue is a life-changing undertaking, even after you find dependable, capable volunteers to help you. It's essentially a full-time, unpaid job. As the founder, the rescue is ultimately your responsibility from start to finish. You will be regularly engaged in computer work, human interactions, canine interactions, daily maintenance activities, vet visits, networking, fundraising, publicity, and much more.

Ask yourself:

- Are you organized?
    - o Being organized is helpful, but if you're naturally a disorganized person, at least recruit an organized treasurer early on to keep your records straight.

- Are you a "people" person?

    o If you are starting a dog rescue to escape humans, you are entering the wrong line of volunteer work. Much of what is involved with running a rescue requires you to deal with people. You need to be able to successfully communicate with volunteers, adopters, board members, etc. If you are not a people person, partner with some people who are great communicators and let them manage volunteers, adopters, events, and other people-related facets of your rescue.

> "What I found my first year in rescue was that rescues tend to lack the human element. Dog rescuers are "dog" people, they're generally not "people" people, and it's very important to our mission that attitude changes."
>
> *–Sharon Sleighter, Legacy Boxer Rescue*

- Can you honestly assess your strengths and weakness?

    o What are you good at? What are you not-so-good at? Make a list, and run it by some trusted friends. Do they agree? To avoid burnout, retain volunteers. Succeeding in rescue requires an understanding of when to participate and when to let others handle things.

- Can you delegate responsibilities?

    o Burnout is one of the biggest challenges of running a rescue. Most founders work full-time jobs and then spend the majority of their "free" time working on their rescue. One way to mitigate burnout and ensure a balanced life is to recruit great volunteers and delegate responsibilities to them. Your rescue will not grow if you hold on to control too tightly.

- Do you have space to house the dogs until you get foster homes?
  - o You will not be able to save every dog who comes your way, and when you begin, you will have limited access to foster homes. Even as you grow, situations will arise where dogs will need temporary shelter and care. Is your family on-board with your starting a rescue? Are your current companion animals? Will you be able to house dogs in your home temporarily or pay for a local boarding facility to house them? (Often local boarding facilities will give discounts to rescue or foster for free. It's worthwhile to begin developing relationships with them early on.)

- Are you in a financial position to support the animals you rescue, at least in the beginning as you develop your rescue?
  - o Veterinary care, grooming, and feeding are not cheap. There will be times, especially before you are incorporated as a 501(c)3 non-profit, that you will need to use your own money to help the dogs in your care. Are you willing and able to do so? Is your family okay with the idea?

- Is your family on board with your decision to start a rescue?
  - o Rescue is going to take up a lot of your time and at least some of your money. Does your family understand that and support your decision to start a rescue? Starting a rescue is not worth losing your family over, as there are always other ways you can help, like volunteering with existing organizations, blogging about pet-related topics, coordinating local adoption events, etc.

- Do you have time to properly care for the rescued dogs, recruit volunteers, arrange transport, attend events, and do the necessary paperwork?
  - o Again, rescue is physically and emotionally consuming. It is a lot of work, and takes a significant amount of time. If you have the time and emotional strength to handle it, rescue is very rewarding, but remember, once you start,

you are responsible for the dogs in your care. Be sure you're available for them.

- Do you have considerable knowledge of the breed(s) you will be rescuing?

  o You will learn as you go, but if you are getting involved with a specific breed, you should learn as much as you can about the breed beforehand. For example, what are common illnesses? Temperament issues? Exercise requirements? This will help you in selecting families for your adoptable dogs and will help you to more quickly identify when veterinary care or special training is needed. Whether you are starting a breed-specific rescue or general rescue, knowledge of training techniques is always useful.

- Do you have any experience in management?

  o Running a rescue means managing volunteers, which can often be more difficult than managing paid employees due to high turnover and low commitment. Experience in management is helpful. If you have never managed people, there are plenty of good books about management available for you to read. Want to save money? Borrow some management books from your local library. Universities, community colleges, Small Business Development Centers (SBDC), and local non-profit assistance organizations often offer management classes. You can find these classes by doing a Google search.

- Are you known for your good instincts and common sense?

  o Working with an existing rescue before starting your own can help you to develop instincts about adopters, volunteers, dogs, etc. Common sense is also helpful, of course, but experience can help you to hone your "gut feelings."

- Are you willing and able to be available whenever a volunteer needs you?

  o There will be times when a foster home has a 2 a.m. crisis, and you'll need to take the call. Can you handle it calmly and coolly at that hour? How will your family handle it? It is imperative that you, as the rescue leader, are readily available when volunteers need you, or you will have a difficult time maintaining volunteers.

- Can you change as your organization changes?

  o As the organization grows, you will need to let go of certain aspects of the organization and trust in volunteers. Are you able to do so? Part of volunteer retention is recognizing your volunteers' self-actualization needs and helping them to flourish. This often means giving them responsibility and allowing them to carry out tasks in the way *they* best see fit. If you are not able to let go of some things as you grow, you might consider instead taking the path of an independent rescuer, taking in dogs and re-homing them on a very small scale.

- Are you good at multitasking?

  o As discussed, running a rescue is a multi-faceted "job." Not only do you need to wear many different hats, but you need to be able to do the "Virginia reel" with a multitude of people and dogs all at once, juggling surrenderers, transport volunteers, fosters, event volunteers, adopters, veterinarians, and of course, dogs, all at once.

- Are you marketing-oriented?

  o One key aspect of rescue is marketing: marketing your dogs to potential adopters and marketing your organization to potential donors. Before you even begin your organization, you should put together a list of fundraising avenues. For ideas, check out *Chapter 7: Fundraising and Donations.*

- Do you have the will to say no to animals for whom you don't have room?

  o Rescuers who aren't careful to guard their emotions and only take in a reasonable number of dogs are at risk of becoming collectors (hoarders). You must condition yourself to understand that *you can't save them all.* What you can do is "just say no" or reach out to other organizations for help.

- Are you prepared to hear the worst of the worst stories of abuse and neglect?

  o Rescue is very rewarding but there is also a very dark, tragic side to it. Most rescuers quickly develop emotional barriers to some of the terrible things they see and hear on a daily basis. How will you deal with your feelings about abuse and neglect? Will you be able to look beyond the hurt and anger to focus on providing the dogs with better lives moving forward?

- If you take in a dog that has incurable health or behavior problems, are you prepared to make a life/death decision on behalf of that dog?

  o Some dogs arrive into rescue fit to be re-homed, while others need veterinary care or behavior modification before they are ready for new forever families. Unfortunately, some dogs are so sick and in pain or so dangerous to society that the only reasonable course of action is euthanization. A rescue founder should never push this decision off on volunteers. You must be strong enough to objectively see what is in the best interest of the dog and your rescue organization to make the tough decisions when necessary.

You might be wondering, "Why would anyone ever get involved in rescue, if it is this hard?" The answer to that is very personal, but you will most likely find that those who are running rescues have felt called to do so, like they had no other choice. Many will tell you that they wish they were more prepared, which is the point of going through this list of questions. If you have any hesitation at all about starting a rescue, get involved with an existing one first. Take up a key volunteer position and see how you like it. If it is in your heart to help dogs, whether you volunteer or found your own rescue, you'll be taking steps in the right direction. There is no rush to found your own organization, so take your time and make sure it is the right thing for you.

Rescue Development Process

Once you've decided that founding a rescue is, indeed, your calling, you should follow a logical process to get started. Founding a rescue isn't as simple as bringing home a stray dog, thinking up a name, and putting an ad on Craigslist because, aside from needing a business structure to attract donors, volunteers, and adopters, without a carefully-planned adoption process, you could be putting the dogs you are trying to save at great risk.

Below are several steps that are necessary in founding a rescue. They do not necessarily have to be completed in this order, but you should set a timeline to accomplish them all:

1. **Finish reading this manual.**

2. Write a business plan.

3. Decide on your rescue structure and find volunteers to fill critical roles.

4. Incorporate your organization, obtain a rescue license (only necessary in some states), and prepare your 501(c)3 paperwork.

5. Set up means of contact (phone number, email, PO box, etc.).

6. Build a website, make a Facebook page, start Tweeting, etc.

7. Develop a relationship with veterinarians.

8. Introduce yourself to local shelters.

9. Research online and local marketing opportunities (Petfinder. com, local adoption events, etc.).

10. Identify and stick to your limitations.

11. Start saving dogs.

Business Plan

Writing a business plan is beyond the scope of this manual, but your local Small Business Development Center (SBDC) or non-profit support agency can help you. Additionally, there are many free examples online. The value of a business plan is that it will help you think through all the aspects of your rescue and prepare you to write the narrative for your 501(c)3 application. Do not skip this step.

501(c)3 Non-Profit Status

Obtaining federal 501(c)3 non-profit status adds legitimacy to your rescue in the eyes of donors and adopters and allows donors to take a write-off on their tax returns when they give you money. Keep in mind, however, that you must stay on top of your bookkeeping to maintain your 501(c)3 status, and you must make your financial statements transparent to the public. Obtaining 501(c)3 status can be a lengthy process, although some filers say it took them less than two months.

A prudent approach is to take in and re-home some animals as you begin preparing your documents. Once you are confident in your ability to find animals loving new homes and your finances are in order, you can file your 501(c)3 paperwork. By taking this pragmatic approach, you'll have an easier time writing the narrative section of your 501(c)3 filing, and you can be sure that spending the fees on filing, which can range from $500 to thousands of dollars, will be a good investment for your organization.

Remember: An animal rescue is a non-profit **business** and must be treated as such to succeed.

What you need:

- Financial resources

  o Filing yourself will cost $450 - $1000+ depending on state filing fees and the projected size of your organization.

  o Having a lawyer file for you can cost thousands more.

  o To save money, look for grants online to help cover the filing fees or become an affiliate of an established organization to avoid the need to file.

- Articles of Organization

- Bylaws

- Conflict of Interest Policy (not always necessary)

- State incorporation

- Federal EIN

- Bookkeeping software

How to file: You must first file Articles of Incorporation (AOI) with your state as a *non-profit corporation*. You will likely need to write a set of bylaws for your organization to complete this step. The next step is to obtain a federal tax identification number (FEIN) from http://irs.gov. Once you have  completed these steps, you can begin the non-profit filing process, which also happens at the IRS website. Note that you will need to name at least three directors in your 501(c)3 application.

Structuring Your Rescue

As a rescue grows, it becomes more dependent on the help of volunteers, but even in the beginning, you'll need a few board members in order to file your 501(c)3 application. Place volunteers in roles that cater to their strengths. Here are some key positions commonly found in rescue organizations:

- **President:** Gives guidance and works with all the different coordinators, makes final decision on matters when necessary, helps in all aspects of the rescue.

- **Vice president:** Fills in for President and helps in all aspects of the rescue when and where needed.

- **Treasurer:** In charge of all financial matters including bill paying, approving expenses, working with the accountant to prepare annual documents, etc.

- **Secretary:** Takes notes at meetings, records names and addresses of donors, sends thank you cards and tax receipts, oversees all office-type work that does not fall to the treasurer.

- **Adoption coordinator:** Reviews applications, speaks with potential adopters, checks references, etc. Helps foster parent approve or disapprove applicants. Coordinates meeting of the dogs with potential adopters if local and coordinates transport if adopters are out of the area. Follows up with adopters after adoptions or ensures fosters follow up with adopters after adoptions. Keeps files of adoption applications and of adoption papers.

- **Event coordinator:** Schedules and promotes events, recruits and manages event volunteers, sets up and takes down tables, promotion items, etc.

- **Fundraising coordinator:** Creates, schedules, promotes, and manages fundraising events; writes grants or manages grant-writing volunteers; works with Treasurer, President, and Vice President to set and achieve fundraising goals.

- **Foster coordinator:** Maintains list of fosters, their dogs, and the dates preventatives and vaccines need to be given; distributes preventatives, medications, and microchips for the foster dogs; serves as primary contact for foster homes regarding questions about foster dogs. Primary liaison with veterinarians (this is sometimes a separate position).

- **Volunteer coordinator:** Recruits volunteers; maintains volunteer list and works with Events Coordinator to contact volunteers for events.*

- **Marketing and promotions coordinator:** Works with Fundraising Coordinator and Events Coordinator to promote the organization at events and to achieve humane education initiatives; creates annual fundraising items such as calendars.

People should only be encouraged to take volunteer positions in which they will be happy to avoid burnout. Rescue is hard work, but that doesn't mean it can't be fun, and the best way to make it fun is to set people up for success, treat them with respect, and support them in their positions. Note that volunteers and board members should not have any financial liability to the organization but they should have access to the organization's financial records.

Legacy Planning

Many rescues will fail without their founders, which is a tragedy for needy dogs and dedicated volunteers alike. As you grow, your responsibility as the founder is to plan for the worst and to ensure the rescue's continuation in your absence. People and pets are counting on you for this. A core group of volunteers along with a capable second-in-command will help ensure continuity in your absence, whether it be short-term or long-term. Hold an annual meeting with key volunteers to discuss the "what-ifs" along with rescue growth, and make sure the people you'd like to have lead the rescue in your absence feel capable to take on leadership roles. Good volunteers are not necessarily good leaders. Rescue leadership commonly requires more than one person, which often manifests as a Board of Directors. The members of the Board should have clear instructions about their expected roles were something to happen to the founder(s).

---

* Please see Chapter 10: Volunteers for further discussion about volunteer positions.

There may also be legal paperwork necessary for leadership to change hands. For example, there should be more than one trusted, registered agent who has access to the rescue's IRS paperwork, bank accounts, etc. Consult a lawyer and/or accountant for further information.

Do:

- DO honestly assess your ability to manage a business and to manage *people.*

- DO consider whether you have the emotional make-up to handle the ups and downs of rescue.

- DO volunteer with another organization or two *before* starting your own.

- DO remain open to the idea that you may be able to do the most good by working with an existing rescue instead of starting your own.

- DO file for 501(c)3 status if you intend to take in donations, have foster homes, participate regularly in adoption events, and advertise your adoptables through online listing services.

- DO apply for grants.

- DO develop a network of volunteers who can share the workload and help you in areas where you lack the appropriate skills and/or enthusiasm to do the job right.

Don't:

- DON'T take in more dogs than you can care for.

- DON'T make rash decisions about founding a rescue.

- DON'T promise write-offs for donations if you don't have your 501(c)3 status.

- DON'T forget to file the appropriate annual paperwork at the state and federal level.

Resources

Rescuers Ring In:
http://upforpups.org/2011/03/best-practices-starting-a-rescue/

Best Friends Start-Up Resources: http://www.bestfriends.org/nomore-homelesspets/resourcelibrary/fororganizations.cfm

How to Start a 501(c)3 Organization: http://www.wikihow.com/Start-a-501c3-Non-profit-Organization

IRS Charities Page: http://www.irs.gov/charities/index.html

Save Ohio Strays Business Plan Synopsis: http://www.saveohiostrays.org/RP_WebDoc.asp?ttid=56

Small Business Development Center: http://www.sba.gov/content/small-business-development-centers-sbdcs

Tax Basics for Exempt Organizations: http://www.stayexempt.irs.gov/

Wikipedia 501(c) information: http://en.wikipedia.org/wiki/501%28c%29

Webster Boneham, Sheila. 2009. Rescue Matters! *How to Find, Foster, and Re-home Companion Animals.* CO: Alpine Publications.

Chapter 4:
Homeless Dogs Needing Help

There is much attention given to the ethics surrounding shelter policies and specifically euthanization, but shelter overcrowding is not the *cause* of dogs ending up homeless and meeting untimely ends. The *cause* is humans irresponsibly breeding dogs when plenty of dogs are already looking for homes. The *cause* is humans not respecting the fact that caring for dogs is a lifetime commitment. The *cause* is a lack of support for low income families to have access to basic veterinary care and spay/neuter surgeries. The *cause* is limited attention given to educating children and adults how to be great pet guardians and what the care of a dog entails. This section covers the various ways animals end up in rescues and how rescues handle dog intake.

Family (Owner) Surrenders

Families become unable to care for their pets for a variety of reasons:

- Job loss

- Foreclosure or loss of housing that causes the family to be forced into pet-unfriendly housing

- Illness or death

- Divorce

- Babies (parents no longer have time to care for the dog or the pet reacts poorly to the new family member)

"When picking up a dog from an owner surrender, we try and reassure the family that they are doing what's best for the dog, whether we agree with why they are giving up their dog or not. We explain how our adoption process works (application, phone interview, home visit, foster home interview) and tell them that we will do our best to find their pet the best place to live."

–Golden Retriever Freedom Rescue, CO

- Family member develops pet allergies

- Major medical expense for dog is too costly

- They just don't want their dog.

- The cute puppy grows up and becomes too big for the family.

Intake Tools

A rescue should have specific paperwork ready for families to fill out and sign before surrendering their dogs. This paperwork should address and protect the interests of both the rescue and the surrendering family.

- Surrender contract

- Intake form

- Experienced volunteer who can pick up the dog and either help the family understand how to keep this from happening again (if applicable) or reassure them they are making the right decision

Surrender contract: All rescues accepting family surrenders should have the family sign a surrender agreement to protect the rescue from the family coming back and saying they didn't mean to surrender their pet and to ensure that the family understands the surrender is final. Contracts can be made available as an online form or printed document, which can be signed and faxed/emailed back or given to the intake volunteer at the time of surrender. Be sure to have a rescue agent's signature on every contract and that both parties receive a copy. A list of specific contract suggestions is located in *Chapter 5: Legal Concerns.*

Intake form: When accepting a family surrender, take advantage of the fact that you can talk to the dog's former family and learn all you can about the pet's history; likes and dislikes; usual sleeping arrangements; and favorite toys, treats, and foods. Having the surrendering family fill out a comprehensive intake form is the best way to ensure the transmission of essential information on to the pet's new foster and forever homes. This also helps the foster family and adopting family make the dog's transition from his or her former home to foster home to forever home as seamless as possible.

> **"One of our family surrenders was in love with chasing a ball. We literally spent two days in our backyard throwing the ball for her. She was in heaven! It made the transition for her much, much easier because we knew what she loved to do and could continue with that." –Kari and Tim Workman, GRFR Foster Parents**

Etiquette: When accepting a family surrender, it is best to give the family the benefit of the doubt that surrendering their pet is very sad and difficult. Families should be treated with respect, even if you don't agree with their motives, because they have given you the power to help place the dog into a better situation. The family will only learn something from this experience and listen to what you have to say if you are nice to them.

In family surrender situations, a rescue may or may not choose to inform the surrendering family when their pet finds a new home. Rescue policies vary about whether or not adopters are encouraged to communicate with the surrendering family. Some rescues choose to handle these situations on a case-by-case basis, depending on the cause of surrender.

Breeder Surrenders

Breeder surrenders are dogs who have been used by a person to make puppies. There are generally three different kinds of breeders from which a rescue receives surrenders:

- Reputable breeders
- Backyard breeders
- Puppy mills

This section discusses what to expect of *typical* dogs coming into your rescue from the following types of breeders. For an explanation of each type of breeder, please see the *Introduction and Definitions* section of this manual.

Reputable breeders: Dogs retired from reputable breeders usually have been properly cared for and socialized. They often have good temperaments and are familiar with life inside a house. These types of breeders also sometimes surrender puppies to rescues if they are "unsellable" because of their age or medical issues or because they don't meet a certain breed standard.

Backyard breeders: The temperament and health of dogs from backyard breeders is highly variable, as backyard breeders range from misled families who want to "show their children the miracle of life" to amateurs who try to make a profit off breeding purebreds and even mutts. Often dogs from backyard breeders have lived their lives in a yard, be they tethered or fenced in, and they sometimes show signs of leash- or fence-aggression because of their former living situations. They are often unsocialized and lack understanding of indoor living rules. Some have medical issues while others are healthy and loving.

Commercial breeding farms (puppy mills): Dogs from puppy mills are often unsocialized and fearful. They do not know how to behave in a home; they are not potty-trained; and they do not respond to a name because they aren't given names in mills. These dogs usually do best when placed in foster homes with other gentle dogs who can "show them the ropes," though some prefer to live without other dogs. Dogs from puppy mills may come into rescue for the following reasons:

- Law enforcement closes a mill because of United States Department of Agriculture (USDA) and/or Animal Welfare Act (AWA) violations.

- The breeder has a relationship with a rescue and relinquishes unproductive dogs "to save a bullet" (an expression used by breeders who would otherwise shoot dogs who are no longer productively breeding).

- Rescue volunteers pose as millers at puppy mill dog auctions, which are state-sanctioned weekly events in several states. These volunteers buy however many auctioned dogs they can to remove the dogs from life in a puppy mill and to ensure the dogs get medical care and good homes. This practice is controversial. Opponents argue that buying the dogs supports puppy mills. Proponents argue that if they don't save the dogs, many will die.

- Rescue volunteers enter mills posing as puppy buyers and then ask to purchase a specific breeding dog instead. The dog in question is usually decided upon by the rescue ahead of time after hearing accounts of a particularly ill or needy dog.

What you need:*

- Surrender contract

- Intake form

Strays and Shelter Dogs

Dogs end up in shelters for many reasons:

- Found as strays

- Surrendered by family or breeder

- Taken from family for abuse or neglect

Shelter dogs have few choices. They are either reclaimed by their guardians, adopted by someone new, euthanized, or picked up by private rescue organizations and put into foster care. *Chapter 2: Rescues and Shelters* has extensive information about how rescues and shelters can work together.

Rescues obtain stray dogs in different ways. They may get a stray directly from a shelter, or a person who finds a stray may call the

---

* *See above "Family Surrender" section for explanations.*

rescue directly. However, if a person calls your rescue about a stray dog, it is better to refer that person to a local shelter. The shelter is usually the first place people call or visit to find and reclaim a lost dog. Stray dogs should be given every opportunity to be reunited with their guardians before being made available for adoption. This is not only a moral obligation, but it is also mandated by state law. Call your local shelter to find out exactly what your state law requires.

As to the condition of strays, some have been on the streets for a long time, so they may be underweight and malnourished, while others look like they were just out on a walk with their guardians. Some have injuries and medical issues, while others are perfectly healthy. One difficulty with strays is that you have no information about their pasts, unless you are able to trace their veterinary care through a rabies tag or find their previous guardian through a microchip. Unfortunately, if the people listed as the contacts no longer want the dog, they will often deny even knowing him or her.

Abuse and Neglect Cases

Sadly, some animals who come in to rescue have been abused or neglected. They may have been chained outside, left in a yard, or stuck in a garage or crate for much of their lives. These dogs' needs vary greatly depending on how they were treated. They may be fearful of people or extremely excited to be in loving homes. Some dogs need rehabilitation before they can learn to trust again.

When your rescue is contacted about any cases where masses of dogs are coming in from a puppy mill bust, a hoarding situation, or a severe neglect case, you must first assess whether your organization has the skills, manpower, housing, and funding necessary to support the recovery of dogs with special needs. Rescuers with a special interest in helping with busts can contact local law enforcement and other groups that already work on cases like this to get information on how these situations are handled locally, what the dogs' needs usually are, and where they can find resources to assist with the care of these types of dogs.

Instances involving lawsuits, such as puppy mill busts, must be handled carefully. Your rescue must work *within* the system until the proper paperwork is completed and the dogs are officially yours. Your rescue must "own" the dogs before you can re-home them. In these situations, before-and-after photos of the dogs and careful recordkeeping are essential.

Intake Coordinators

Rescues usually designate one specific person to communicate with families surrendering dogs because they often need more hand-holding than shelter-transfer or puppy mill surrender cases. The volunteer designated for this task must be patient and interested in taking the potential surrenderer from inquiry to surrender—the whole way. That volunteer should ensure the rescue receives all essential paperwork from the surrenderer, including the surrender contract, intake forms, and veterinary records. Many rescues request a surrender donation (often $50-$100) but do not require it.

Depending on the percentage of dogs who come in from each different segment, rescues may have different intake coordinators. They may have one for puppy mill relinquishes, one for shelter transfers, one for strays, etc. Whatever the case, the intake coordinator is responsible for gathering pertinent information about each dog, finding a suitable foster home (often working with the foster coordinator on this), and collaborating with the transport coordinator when necessary.

Intake Policies

It is very difficult to say "no" to a dog in need, but nothing is worse than having your rescue commit to taking in an animal and then doing no better for that precious pet than what the former neglectful owner had been doing. The fact is that no matter how many animals you take in, there are still going to be millions more (literally) you will not be able to save. To help you avoid taking in more dogs than you can handle, create a clear, written intake policy that answers the following questions:

- Who handles intake phone calls?

- Who makes the ultimate decision on intakes?

- Do dogs from certain situations get priority?

  o Example: Many rescues put family surrenders below puppy mill dogs or urgent shelter pulls.

- How many dogs can you handle at a time?

  o Budget concerns

  o Number of open foster homes

  o Expected monthly adoption application volume

- What are the basic care items you provide for each dog before it goes to a forever home?

- What will cause the rescue to determine a dog is unadoptable (certain health issues?)

- What will you do if the dog you take in has a serious medical concern? Do you have a mechanism to raise additional funds for veterinary care?

Intake policies vary among rescues. Some groups take in any dog who fits their parameters, while others have a waiting list. It can't be stressed enough that you should only take in the number of animals you are reasonably capable of caring for. Some rescues choose to immediately take in dogs from dangerous situations, like puppy mill surrenders and abuse/neglect cases, while asking families who want to surrender their dogs to wait until they have more space if necessary. Alternatively, for less urgent cases, a rescue may offer to post "courtesy listings" for family surrender, keeping the animal in the original home until a new family is found. Some rescues have relationships with local boarding facilities for dogs in emergency situations.

All rescues require some manner of intake paperwork for every dog who comes into their care. The paperwork includes a surrender contract and an intake form detailing the dog's history, reasons why dog is being relinquished, and the dog's medical and behavioral history.

Rescues need a clearly defined evaluation process for incoming dogs. Holding and evaluation periods vary among rescues, but a good policy allows time for an evaluator to observe the following issues:

- Physical check

  o fleas/ticks/lice

  o ear mites

  o obvious injuries

  o spay/neuter

- Temperament check

  o Resource guarding (food, toys, crates)

  o Aggression toward other animals or humans

Evaluating an incoming dog can be difficult because the dog's past must be taken into account. If the dog just came out of a shelter, for example, there is a good chance that he or she is *freaked out* from the shelter environment and possibly is acting differently than he or she normally would. Even dogs who come from loving families may experience separation anxiety upon surrender. Dogs should be treated as individuals and evaluated as such. Some temperament evaluation tests are available online. One place to start is the American Temperament Test Society. It is very important to evaluate dogs on an individual basis, and the evaluation should be done before dogs goes into a foster home, if possible, to ensure they are placed with the appropriate family (okay with cats vs. no cats, okay with kids vs. no kids, needs quiet, etc.).

"Just like with people, no dog is perfect. However, there are as many people who are inclined to adopt "less perfect" dogs as there are people who want puppies. Do not be too quick to deem a dog "unadoptable." Your foster families play a key role in helping dogs through their fears and issues, and as long as the dog does not have real, unmanageable health or behavioral issues, that dog can most likely be placed in a forever home. – *Shereen Raucci, Mile High Weimaraner Rescue*

Identification

Many dogs who come into rescue are a flight risk. They are nervous, disoriented, and at times, temporarily inconsolable. All rescues lose dogs from time to time, but with the help of microchips, dogs and rescues are often reunited. Buying your chips directly from organizations like Home Again, Avid, and 24Petwatch makes it easier and less expensive for you. (In bulk they should cost approximately $5 each.) When you buy them directly, the microchip organization usually automatically records your rescue's information as the contact to call when the dog is found, even before the chips are ever injected into your dogs. Having your rescue listed as a contact is important not only while the dog is in foster care but also after he or she has been adopted because in the event that a dog is found and the family contact information is out of date or unregistered, the chip will lead the person who found the dog back to you. Rescues normally add the adopter as the primary contact several weeks after the dog has been adopted to make sure that the adoption is going to last and that the chip actually does get registered.

Microchips should be inserted by trained veterinary technicians.

While most dogs in rescue get microchipped, many municipalities also require that dogs have identification tags. Some rescues provide tags to foster homes with the rescue's phone number on them. Most rescues require foster families to always keep a collar with identification tags on their foster dogs, even if the rescue uses harnesses for walking. These tags and collars can be transferred from foster dog to foster dog as dogs are adopted out and new ones come in.

Adopted and Returned

Many rescues have some sort of trial period, in which a person can return a dog and receive a refund. This is discussed in detail in *Chapter 12: Adoption Process.* Rescues take great care in placing the right dog with the right family, but sometimes, for a variety of reasons, the adoption doesn't work out. Often, if an adoption is going to fall through because of compatibility issues, it does so in the first few days, but sometimes a dog will come back into rescue after being adopted for months or years. If a dog is returned after a significant time has lapsed, a refund and/or replacement is generally not issued. However, a person returning a dog should not be chastised for the return. After all, he or she is at least upholding the tenants of the adoption contract, which is discussed in detail later in this manual. If and the situation requires you to educate a person about how to not end up having to surrender a dog in the future, address it delicately. Most often there is really nothing to address (for example, if the guardian gets sick and has nobody to care for the dog). When a dog is returned, a volunteer should reevaluate the dog, noting any changes from when the dog was previously in foster care. Most rescues then move the dog to the top of the list of adoptables.

If you have a dog who is continuously adopted and returned, consider whether the dog would be better served by a different rescue. This is especially the case with mixed-breed dogs. For example, a Golden Retriever Rescue that takes in a Golden Retriever/ Border Collie mix who is strongly herding-oriented would do well to consider calling a cattle dog rescue for help. Prioritize helping other rescues with similar issues, as you never know when you're going to need their help, such as in the aforementioned situation.

Do:

- DO treat breeders, surrenderers, and others with respect—at least they are giving your rescue the dog.

- DO outline intake procedures and follow them.

- DO decide on a dog evaluation policy.

- DO get to know your foster families (i.e. number and ages of kids, other dogs, cats, pets in the house; lifestyle, etc.).

- DO share and reinforce policies with volunteers.

- DO have a trial period policy and a return policy that does not encourage people to second-guess their decision for financial reasons.

- DO microchip all of the dogs who come into your rescue.

Don't:

- DON'T take in more dogs than your rescue can care for.

- DON'T ignore legal issues with cases involving raids and animal control.

- DON'T be rude to people relinquishing their dogs or to adopters who return their dogs.

Resources

Rescuers Ring In: http://upforpups.org/2011/03/best-practices-homeless-pets-needing-help/

ASPCA Humane Law Enforcement Agent Information (NY Only): http://www.aspca.org/fight-animal-cruelty/animal-precinct/become-an-hle-officer.aspx

America Temperament Test Society: http://www.atts.org/testdesc.html

Microchip Companies:

   Home Again: http://public.homeagain.com/

   Avid: http://www.avidid.com/

   24PetWatch: http://www.24petwatch.com/

Chapter 5:
Legal Concerns

To maintain non-profit status and protect your organization from legal exposure, all rescues should document all their processes and procedures. Rescues must have liability insurance. If a dog bites someone or a volunteer is injured and the rescue is sued, it needs basic coverage. At the very least, your rescue needs pet liability insurance. A legal advisor well-versed in non-profit and animal welfare law can be immeasurably helpful to you and your rescue in determining what type of insurance your organization needs and what legal issues you should be aware of. It is also a good idea to get an accountant who knows non-profit accounting and to develop a good relationship with an insurance agent who can guide you in procuring the appropriate insurance policies.

There are several legal issues to consider when you accept a dog into your organization. If your rescue takes in a stray dog, make sure a volunteer reports him or her to local animal control agencies and that you make the dog available for reclamation for the minimum number of days required by your local laws. In the case of surrenders, be sure the surrenderer signs a contract indicating willful surrender of the dog and reveals any known "issues" the animal may have.

Additionally, be sure foster agreements acknowledge that the rescue cannot be held liable for damage a dog does to people or their homes, that the dog is legally in the *rescue's care,* and that any of the rescue's property will be returned in good condition when the foster volunteer no longer wishes to continue as a foster or is dismissed from volunteering with the rescue. It's also a good idea to ask foster homes to carry their own liability insurance. Some rescues do criminal background checks on volunteers. If minors want to volunteer, parents must sign a waiver.

Once a contract is completed, the rescue should scan and file it electronically in addition to keeping a hard copy for a specified period of time. This is usually the duty of the board secretary.

"Dangerous" Dogs

Labeling a treatable dog as "aggressive" or "dangerous" is a sure way to set him or her up for adoption failure. Some rescuers feel these terms misplace blame and suggest that "insecure" would be a better term. "Insecure" doesn't create the same bad label for the dog and encourages empathy instead of blame. The term "insecure" also infers a solution, whereas "aggressive" does not.

Many terms thrown around to describe insecure dogs are subjective and easy to misinterpret, which is why it is very important for every rescue to have a clear dog-aggression/dog-bite policy. The policy should both define these terms and list a clear process on how to deal with them. Defining "aggressive behavior" can be difficult because what is perceived as aggressive for a Dachshund may be perceived as completely normal for a Border Collie. Border Collies regularly nip at other dogs and people as part of their hard-wired herding behavior; Dachshunds are not herders and therefore should not normally behave in that way.

To complicate the issue, aggressive behavior may be situational. Some dogs may be leash aggressive but calm when off-leash. Other dogs may appear aggressive in a kennel but are simply acting out of fear. For this reason, a dog should be given more than one chance, if possible, and all rescues should strive to set their dogs up for success. For example, if a dog is acting out in one situation, he or she should be tested in other situations before being sentenced to death for aggressive behavior.

To determine what the term "dangerous" truly means to your rescue, you must consider your state's legal definitions of "dangerous" or "vicious" and read up on dog bite laws. These laws will relate to bite history or even breed. Some states still have a one-bite rule. Understanding these laws will help you to avoid lawsuits.

Reputable rescues make every effort within their means to avoid euthanizing a dog. This includes rehabilitating bad behavior and testing for health issues that may cause aggression. A rescue should use euthanization only as a last resort for dogs who pose a real, unmanageable threat to society. A dog who can be trained is not dangerous and should not be euthanized. An example of this is a large breed dog who jumps on people and knocks them over. This is not an aggression issue, and it can be handled with training and the careful selection of forever homes (e.g., not re-homing a rambunctious dog to a family with small children).

> "We recently received a young Weim who had suffered prior physical abuse and probably being chained. The first three months in rescue, he had to wear a muzzle in public. With the help of a trainer and very dedicated foster parents, he has been successfully adopted. We did, however, mandate that the adopters complete an eight-week course with that same trainer before the adoption would be finalized. I got to see the Weim last weekend with his new family, and the change is amazing." *–Shereen Raucci, Mile High Weimaraner Rescue*

While one cannot speculate a concrete time frame for evaluating a dog because every dog is different, a rescue can develop an evaluation *process.* Having a defined process can help evaluate dogs more efficiently and fairly. A Google search for "dog temperament test" reveals many different ideas on how to temperament test a dog. Additionally, consider partnering with a local dog trainer or behaviorist to develop a fair testing system that works best for your rescue. If you have a good process, your more experienced foster homes can be a good resource to help determine whether a dog can be rehabilitated, but if you have a questionable dog, be sure to place him or her with a foster who is aware of the risks and can handle the responsibility.

Euthanization is never an easy decision, but ethically the call must be made if all other efforts to change the dog's aggressive behavior have failed. Rescues also have to consider the liability of so-called dangerous dogs because if an adopter or other person is bitten maliciously, and that person files a lawsuit, your rescue will likely lose. This is a disservice to all the dogs who will not be saved because of the one dog who bit someone. If a dog has a trigger, then those triggers can be avoided or work can be done to desensitize the dog to that trigger. But if there really is no warning, no professional can figure out a trigger, the dog cannot be distracted or interrupted during an attack, or attacking another dog is fun for the attacker (very rare), euthanization is likely unavoidable.

> **"If you stay in rescue long enough, there will come a time that you will have to make (one of) the hardest decision(s) in your life. My thought on the subject is there is a difference between life and quality of life. This difficult decision should be made as a group, including your veterinarian and possibly a behaviorist and a trainer, depending on the circumstance. It will be a hard decision to make, but it should be what you collectively feel is best for the animal and the community." –Linda Sutphin, Dogs 2ⁿᵈ Chance**

Euthanasia decisions are an example of a circumstance when it is helpful to have a strong Board of Directors or other advisory group. Some rescues feel the decision to euthanize should be made by a board. Board decisions tend to be less biased and also disperse the guilt such a decision may cause.

Contracts

Adoption contracts, fostering agreements, and surrender forms are discussed in their respective chapters.

Taking Donations

Donors may only take a write-off for their donations to your organization if you have been approved as a non-profit entity on the federal level. If your rescue has its 501(c)3 status, it is a legal non-profit entity. A "tax deductible" donation is one that is made to a tax-exempt organization, and the donor receives nothing in return.

The following are **not** eligible for a tax deduction:

- Adoption fees (depends on your state laws)
- Purchase of raffle tickets/chances
- Auction items
- On donations resulting in a "free gift," donors may only deduct the difference between what they donated and the value of the gift.

The following items **are** eligible for a tax deduction:

- The known value of donated items (used or new)
- Gift certificate for the value amount
- Monetary donation
- Gas value when transporting a dog (check with your accountant on how to calculate this)

It's good to accept donations of items, even if your rescue doesn't need these items. Donors are turned off when they offer something for free and the recipient denies it. The result is that next time, when the item may be just what your rescue needed, it may not be offered to you. If you receive a donated item that you know your rescue cannot use, accept it and then donate it to another group, or use it as a prize at a fundraising event.

Respond to donations with a thank-you note and receipt confirming the donation. The receipt should include a description of the donation, including the name of the donated item and the value, the donor's name and address, and the date of the donation. If the donation is an item (as opposed to money), leave a blank line for the donor to fill in the market value. Include information about what the donation will be used for, the rescue's contact information, and the rescue's FEIN (tax identification number given to the organization by the IRS).

The importance of donor relationships can't be stressed enough. Some organizations recognize donors who wish to be recognized (many wish to remain anonymous) in their newsletters and on their websites. Most organizations also send thank-you notes to donors. This task can be designated to a volunteer who writes the notes and submits monthly reports showing when thank-you notes were sent and to whom to ensure timely execution. The organization should provide the note cards, envelopes, and postage. Custom thank-you notes are available online inexpensively and are a nice touch.

There are many different avenues rescues can use to solicit donations. These are outlined in *Chapter 7: Fundraising and Donations.*

Filing and Recordkeeping

Non-profit organizations are required by law to generate an annual financial report when they file taxes, and a non-profit dog rescue is no exception. Using the computer program, QuickBooks, is a great way to keep track of all the rescue's finances (QuickBooks even has a non-profit version). A rescue should plan on spending at least 94% of its revenue on programs associated with its mission (intake, veterinary care, outreach, etc.). Check with your accounting for more information about this.

As of the publication of this manual, small rescues generating less than $50,000 in income and donations only need to file a 990-N e-Postcard annually with the IRS. Larger organizations need to file a form 990 or 990-EZ annually. State filing requirements vary. Check with your accountant.

Disclosures

A rescue should be transparent when it comes to disclosures to adopters, volunteers, and donors. With adopters and volunteers, it never pays to be misleading because a failure to share all of a dog's history increases the likelihood of that dog being returned or a volunteer quitting and badmouthing you and the rescue. Being direct and upfront from the start fosters trust and loyalty. If it's not a good match, it's better to admit it.

Foster parent disclosures: A rescue should require its foster parents to complete a foster application and contract that states the foster's responsibilities as well as the organization's responsibilities. Items to address include:

- Food supply (whether the foster parent or the rescue supplies the food; brand of food)

- Crate/bedding

- Transport/gas to and from the vet and to adoptive family

- Medical and maintenance costs (reimbursement or organization pays the vet/groomer directly)

- Training requirements for the foster parent to conduct

- Emergency plans

- Vacations/time off

- Other supplies: grooming, toys, belly bands/diapers, harness/collar, leash, winter coats

- Liability
  - o   If the foster dog is lost or stolen
  - o   Death of the pet
  - o   Attacks and bites to personal dogs and people
  - o   Inspections of the foster home
  - o   Specific grounds for foster termination

- Foster Adoption

    o Policy on foster families adopting foster dogs

    o Often jokingly termed "foster failure"

- Basic verbiage

    o "This Agreement is made and entered into on (DATE) by and between (Organization Name) and the following individuals(s) (Foster Parent Names), (hereinafter 'Foster')."

Note: Many rescues require foster parents to initial each line to ensure they have read each bullet.

Family surrender disclosures: People surrendering dogs to your organization must be made aware of your rescue's re-homing program and evaluation process. The surrenderer should sign a form that includes

- Validation that the surrenderer is the legal guardian of the animal and is surrendering the animal of his or her own free will.

- A policy stating that contact information of the surrenderer and of the new adopting family will not be shared between one another, unless specifically requested by surrenderer and agreed to by adopter.

- An evaluation process and reclamation policy.

    o Does the surrenderer want to be notified if the rescue deems the dog unadoptable? Does the rescue allow surrenderers to reclaim their dogs?

- A request for any known issues.

    o Surrenderer should indicate any "issues" the dog has.

o   Surrenderer should acknowledge that he or she has fully informed the organization of all known or suspected problems and concerns about this animal.

Do:

- DO be sure your rescue has a way of documenting all its processes and procedures and keeps track of all financial transactions.

- DO have a policy on how to evaluate and determine if a surrendered dog is adoptable and what to do if it isn't.

- DO provide a proper donation receipt to donors along with a thank-you note.

- DO develop a foster parent application and contract that indicates the foster's and the rescue's responsibilities.

- DO utilize a family surrender form that requests proof the surrenderer is the legal owner, vaccinations and veterinary records, and information about the dog's habits, likes/ dislikes, and issues (food aggression, barking in appropriately, nervous, etc.).

Don't:

- DON'T forget to get liability insurance for your rescue.

- DON'T shortchange your rescue by not creating the proper forms necessary for adoptions, surrenders, and foster homes.

- DON'T label a dog as aggressive without going through proper chanels with your vet or a professional dog handler to have the dog assessed.

- DON'T turn down a donated item. If your rescue can't use it, a different rescue can.

- DON'T try to hide negative information about a dog from fosters and adopters.

Resources

Rescuers Ring In: http://upforpups.org/2011/03/best-practices-legal-concerns-dangerous-animals/

Rescuers Ring In (Part 2): http://upforpups.org/2011/03/best-practices-legal-concerns-part-2/

Dog Bite Law: http://dogbitelaw.com/

Dog Law: http://www.animallaw.info/articles/armpusstatedoglaws.htm

Managing Liability in Animal Rescue Organizations: http://network.bestfriends.org/initiatives/pitbulls/news.aspx?pID=11918

Insurance Group USA (rescue insurance): http://www.insurancegroupusa.com/insurancegroupusa/animalrescue.jsp

Chapter 6:
Veterinary Care

Having the financial means to cover veterinary care is a major concern to most rescue groups. Even established 501[c]3 animal rescues have never-ending vet bills. In general, adoption fees don't begin to cover a rescue's annual veterinary expenses, let alone additional costs. That's why rescuers mainly rely on donations to keep rescuing. Dogs who come into rescue should be provided with medical care, but at times it does become necessary to draw a line. A rescuer must consider a dog's quality of life and likelihood of survival as well as the overall financial state of the rescue before committing to expensive surgeries and treatments. If a dog is terminally ill, it may be enough for a foster home to provide the best quality of life possible while the dog lives out the last of his or her days.

Choosing a Veterinarian

Rescue groups receive dogs from many different environments. Dogs coming into your rescue may have been exposed to viruses, parasites, or other diseases prior to their arrival. These dogs may be ill or incubating disease. Many dogs are not spayed/neutered or up to date on shots. A desperate need for dental care is also very common. Whatever the issues, once you take in a dog, proper veterinary care for that animal becomes your responsibility.

In some locations, local vets may offer rescues a discount (usually 10-25%, but some offer as much as 50%). Some towns also have low cost veterinary clinics, which may turn out to be even cheaper than the discount your local veterinarian offers you. Seek out at least two or three low cost veterinarians and establish a good working relationship with them. The reason you want more than one veterinary partner is that things can change rather quickly if a veterinary hospital changes ownership or institutes new policies. You don't want to be left at the last minute without options, and you also don't want to "wear out the welcome mat" of those who have offered to help you. Meet with the managers of the clinics in person (taking them to lunch is a great idea). Discuss the clinics' procedures and costs, and prepare a checklist that authorizes the routine items you will want done on each new intake. Get a written price list from them so that you can prepare a budget, and make sure they understand and agree with your group's ethics and ideology (e.g., agree ahead of time on what to do if the veterinarian goes to spay a dog and discovers she is pregnant).

When it's necessary to have surgery performed on a foster dog, your veterinarian will ask whether you want pre-surgical diagnostics on the dog. Some rescues forego these completely because of the expense. Others leave the decision up to their veterinarian's discretion. Some rescues adopt a policy of only running diagnostics on dogs older than a certain age. Most rescues do not have pre-surgical diagnostics run on *every* dog who needs surgery. Don't be shy about getting a second or third opinion and price quote from other veterinary clinics, and carefully discuss the "what-ifs" with each veterinarian. If your rescue can't afford the recommended care, find out what alternatives are available and what they cost.

A great relationship with a veterinarian is extremely important, so treat your veterinarians with respect and appreciation. They are not obligated to give you discounted services and freebies, and occasional acknowledgements of their generosity can go a long way. Most rescues regularly thank their veterinarians (at least during the holidays) with home-baked cookies, items representative of the animals they rescue, or at the very least, sincere thank-you notes. They also advertise the veterinarian's practice on their website, in newsletters, and in adoption kits. Though no rescue should require adopters to use their veterinarians, there is nothing wrong with recommending competent veterinarians who help your organization.

Emergency Medical Care

Medical emergencies for foster dogs can happen at any time. To give a dog the best chance of survival in an emergency, rescues need a policy that allows fosters to spend up to a certain amount, say $800, in emergency situations without having to first get the expense approved.

Common Medical Concerns:*

Many rescuers, especially those who run breed-specific rescues, become very familiar with common dog ailments. They can often buy wholesale medications and preventatives, such as heartworm pills, with the help of their veterinarians. Some common medications that rescues keep on hand include Drontal® (a dewormer), Clavamox®, Rimadyl® and Baytril®. Medications should not be administered without veterinary oversight.

Rescuers should address and treat the known medical issues of all dogs in their care before sending them to forever homes. All past and present medical issues should be disclosed to potential adopters, including monthly treatment costs for ongoing issues that cannot be cured before the animal is re-homed. At the very least, rescues should bring a dog up to date on core vaccines, spay/neuter the dog, and care for life-threatening issues (such as heartworm) before a dog is adopted. Make every attempt to treat the rescued dogs just as you would your personal canine companions.

The following is a partial list of veterinary care-related items you may encounter:

Allergies: Some breeds are more prone to allergies than others. Allergies may occur in response to fleas, food, or exposure to things in the environment (pollens, grasses, dust mites, etc.). Symptoms include excessive itching, licking, scratching, and hair loss. Some dogs with food allergies develop diarrhea and may vomit in addition to having skin issues. Diet variations and supplements like fatty acids can help with food allergies. With other types of allergies, frequent bathing can help. If fleas are present, proper flea control must be instituted. Seek veterinary care for any dog who is itchy to the point of discomfort and hair loss.

Arthritis: Arthritis is common in older dogs. If untreated, arthritis can cause debilitating pain. Arthritis cannot be reversed or prevented, but its effects can be minimized with medications like Rimadyl®,

---

* Consult a veterinarian before treating any animal for medical concerns.

tramadol, and gabapentin. Glucosamine and other joint supplements can also help lessen or slow the progression of arthritis. Many vets recommend adding turmeric to a dog's diet as well, since this herb is known to lessen inflammation. Daily, easy exercise is important for a dog with arthritis because it helps keep the blood flowing and the muscles strong.

Diarrhea: This is very common and can be due to the stress of being in a new environment, change in diet, or myriad other factors. Usually diarrhea resolves itself in a few days, but a bland diet such as boiled chicken mixed with canned pumpkin, cottage cheese, or cooked rice can help. Dogs can take Pepto-Bismol or Kaopectate, but be sure to check with your vet for the correct dosage. Probiotics such as Fortiflora®, Prostora®, and similar products can also help promote gastro-intestinal health and treat diarrhea resulting from stress, change in diet, or similar causes. IMPORTANT: Be sure the affected dog is drinking enough water, so he or she does not become dehydrated. Dehydration can occur quickly, especially if a dog is malnourished, has underlying health issues, or is a small-breed dog. If the dog shows signs of dehydration, has bloody stools, or has diarrhea that continues for three or more days, contact a veterinarian.

Distemper: Distemper is also a viral disease, and like parvovirus, it tends to be most serious in puppies and young dogs. Symptoms include gastrointestinal signs such as vomiting and diarrhea; respiratory symptoms such as coughing, sneezing, and runny nose; and central nervous system signs including seizures and coma. Distemper is quite frequently fatal and is extremely contagious to other dogs. Treatment is symptomatic and often not successful in saving the infected puppy. This virus is easily prevented with appropriate vaccination.

Ear infections: Ear infections are more common in some breeds than others, but left untreated they can cause hearing loss. They can also be extremely painful. Symptoms of an ear infection include a discharge or an odor from the ears. Dogs with ear infections often shake their heads and scratch at their ears, sometimes to the point of causing hair loss and sores around the ears. Ears should be cleaned with a cleaning solution and cotton balls or gauze pads as needed. The use of Q-tips is not recommended. If the inside of the dog's ears are red, oozing, smelly, or dirty, or if you suspect the dog has an ear infection, consult a veterinarian for advice on additional treatment.

Fleas/ticks: Examine your foster dogs regularly for fleas and ticks. The propensity of fleas and ticks and the diseases they carry varies across the nation, but in some areas, fleas and ticks carry life-threatening illnesses. Consult with a vet to find out the protocol in your area.

Heartworm: Although heartworm is easily prevented with a monthly pill, many dogs come to a rescue heartworm positive (HW+). A simple blood test can determine whether a dog is infected with heartworms. Numerous tableside tests are available that provide results in 10 minutes or less. Heartworm is transmitted by an infected mosquito and is most common in the Midwest and southern states. Unfortunately, heartworm is becoming more widespread. While the cost of prevention is reasonable, treatment of a HW+ dog is very expensive ($500 - $3,000) and is very difficult for the dog. There are several different ways to treat heartworm, but most commonly dogs are injected with two or more treatments of Immiticide®, a poison that kills the worms. Because the worms break up into small pieces that can cause clots in the heart and lungs, dogs must maintain very little activity during the course of treatment, or they risk death. This means keeping HW+ dogs who are going through treatment crated inside the home and taking them only on slow, leashed walks for a period of at least a month or two (confinement periods vary depending on the course of treatment). Vets *all over the country* as well as the American Heartworm Society recommend keeping a dog on a heartworm preventative year round because it prevents against other parasites in addition to heartworm and because of the severity of the disease.

Mange: Mange can be caused by different species of mites, some of which are more contagious than others. In dogs, demodectic mange is most common, but sarcoptic mange is also possible. Other forms of mange exist as well. Dogs with mange may claw furiously at their skin or bite at themselves, which often results in oozing sores that can lead to secondary infection. In addition to the itching, hair loss is a possible indicator of mange. Ivermectin, medicated baths, and antibiotics are often used to treat dogs with mange. Dogs with skin conditions should be taken to a veterinarian because allergies, mange, and other skin issues tend to have similar symptoms. Some forms of mange, particularly sarcoptic mange, are contagious to people as well as to other dogs.

Obesity: Obesity can be life-threatening in dogs. Veterinarians estimate that over 50% of the pets seen in the United States are overweight or obese. Foster homes should be trained to care for obese dogs and adoption coordinators should counsel adopters about how to evaluate a dog's body condition and how to keep him or her fit (or help the dog become fit). Treatment for severe obesity should be overseen by a veterinarian, since it may be caused by something other than overeating and lack of exercise. Many rescuers use green beans and other vegetables to substitute a portion of a dog's dry food as part of a weight-loss plan. These help the dog to feel full on fewer calories, which usually results in weight loss. Swimming with a life jacket on can also help a dog to safely lose weight because it doesn't cause stress on the dog's joints like jogging will.

Parvovirus: Parvovirus, sometimes simply called "parvo," is a virus that attacks the intestinal tract of dogs. It most commonly affects puppies and young dogs but can be seen on occasion in adult dogs as well. Symptoms include vomiting, diarrhea (often bloody), lack of appetite, depression, fever, and dehydration. Parvovirus is a potentially deadly virus, especially for puppies. There is no cure for parvovirus and treatment is limited. Fluid therapy, usually intravenous, is necessary to battle dehydration. Antibiotics and anti-nausea medications are also used as necessary in treatment. Aggressive treatment is usually necessary to save a dog with parvovirus, but even with treatment, many do not survive. Parvovirus is extremely contagious to unprotected dogs and is spread through contact with infected feces. This virus is easily prevented with appropriate vaccination.

Ringworm: Ringworm is a fungal disease that affects the skin of infected dogs. Despite its name, ringworm is not caused by a worm, and it should not be confused with roundworms (which are intestinal worms). Ringworm causes hair loss and itchiness. It is extremely contagious to both pets and people. Do not re-home dogs with ringworm until the ringworm lesions are controlled because the disease is contagious and difficult to treat. Treatment may involve antifungal medications such as ketaconazole (given orally), medicated baths, and ointments. Clean the pet's environment thoroughly and regularly even after the symptoms subside. Animals can become re-infected by contamination present in the home or shelter.

Spay/neuter: Many dogs arrive intact, which means they haven't been spayed or neutered. Spaying and neutering is extremely important, and in most parts of the country, you can find a clinic that will spay/neuter dogs for less than $100. Spaying and neutering prevents unwanted litters, reduces the risk of other health issues, decreases marking and other undesirable behaviors in many dogs, and generally makes it more likely for a dog to get along with other dogs. All rescues should spay/neuter their dogs before adopting them out unless a medical issue or very young age prevents an animal from safely undergoing the procedure. In that case, rescues can require adopters to provide a pre-paid spay/neuter receipt from the vet or a deposit to the rescue that will be returned once the dog undergoes the procedure. Currently, many rescues are spaying and neutering dogs as young as six-to-eight weeks of age.

Vaccinations: Dogs are vaccinated to protect both the individual dog and other dogs around them. Some diseases we vaccinate against, such as parvovirus, can be deadly, and an outbreak could cause the deaths of many animals. Core vaccinations are those vaccines that protect against diseases that are either particularly serious for an infected dog or are dangerous to the people and dogs around the infected animal. These vaccines include distemper, parvovirus, adenovirus, and rabies. Core vaccines are recommended for all dogs. Dogs *must* have their rabies vaccination before crossing state lines for transport.

Some vaccines, like *Bordetella,* are elective since they protect against viruses that are either extremely unlikely or merely an inconvenience. These are known as non-core vaccines. Non-core vaccines should be administered based on an evaluation of whether the risk of the particular disease outweighs the risk of the vaccination for the individual dog. Besides *Bordetella,* other examples of non-core vaccines include those against leptospirosis, coronavirus, Lyme disease, and snake venom.

Vaccines can be purchased online. However, it is important that you purchase them from a reputable website and take great caution in administering your own vaccines to your rescued dogs. Even if you purchase vaccines online, it is usually better to have your vet administer them. If your rescue does administer vaccines itself, create a form for vaccines with your rescue information on it and a place to put the stickers from the vials after vaccinating the rescue pet. Give this form to the dog's new adopted family.

Worms/parasites: The most common intestinal worms seen in dogs are roundworms, hookworms, whipworms, and tapeworms, depending on the geographic region from which the dog comes. Other intestinal parasites include coccidia and giardia. Worms/parasites can be treated with an appropriate dewormer. The choice of medication will vary depending on the type of parasite. Some types of parasites may need to be treated two to three times at two-to-four week intervals in order to completely eradicate all life stages of the parasite. It is important to pick up feces immediately from a dog who has worms to ensure the worms don't spread. Most worms live in the soil and are transmitted when other dogs step in the contaminated area and then groom themselves. Tapeworms, however, require an intermediate host to pass them on, which is usually a flea or small prey animal. Dogs with worms should be treated immediately because the worms can cause gastro-intestinal issues, weight loss, diarrhea, vomiting, etc. Worms like roundworms and hookworms are also contagious to people. Rescues in areas where there is a high incidence of intestinal worms often decide to forgo fecal exams on their dogs and instead treat all incoming dogs with a dewormer medication.

At least one or two core members of your rescue should be well versed in the common medical issues associated with your breed (purebred rescue) or dogs in general (all-breed rescue). A reference document listing common illnesses/issues and your rescue's procedure is a helpful inclusion in a foster welcome kit. Never assume that your average pet guardian/foster home is knowledgeable about common health issues, especially those diseases frequently seen in rescued animals.

Difficult Decisions

If your rescue is contacted about taking in a dog with medical issues, you should first find out the expenses associated with treating the dog before agreeing to take him or her into your care. For example, if you are approached about a dog with a broken limb, you can assume that care will cost at least $500. However, depending on the severity, the cost could be $2,000 or more. Once you have committed to taking the animal, you have committed to caring for him or her as needed. Unfortunately, you will not know what that entails until your veterinarian has examined the animal. If a simple splint and crate rest is all that is necessary, count your blessings. Many fractures require surgery from an often-expensive specialty veterinarian or orthopedic surgeon. Most general practice veterinarians cannot perform this type of surgery. So, if you only have $1,000 to commit to that animal, you may want to consider passing on this dog and rescuing another one or launching a massive fundraiser to pay for that animal's care.

Your rescue also needs a policy for taking in dogs with terminal or incurable illnesses. Obviously, adopting a dog with a terminal illness is not an option for most people. Therefore, many rescues look to their foster homes to provide hospice care for terminal cases. Hospice care can be defined as care to keep the animal comfortable, with a good quality of life, until that is no longer sustainable. Often this requires minimal expense to the rescue, as long as you are committed to quality of life without heroic efforts to try to save the animal as the disease progresses. Many dogs with cancer fall into this category, as do dogs with severe hip dysplasia and degenerative myelopathy, for example. Before taking in a terminally ill dog, however, your rescue needs to consider whether it can spare a foster home for a dog who won't be adopted. If you have a limited number of foster homes, your rescue may not want to occupy them with dogs who aren't adoptable. An alternative may be to refer the surrenderer to an animal sanctuary like Best Friends (http://bestfriends.org) in Utah, where the dog can comfortably live out his or her life without causing you to have a shortage of foster homes.

Behavioral issues need to be addressed before dogs are adopted out. Three common behavioral issues seen in rescue animals, all of which *usually* manifest from insecurities, include separation anxiety, animal aggression, and to a lesser extent, human aggression. Dogs with these issues are difficult to place, and in some cases, impossible. Therefore, you need policies on how your rescue will handle these challenges, even though each case will be individually evaluated. Having a basic plan and proper policies will help you to better decide what is to be done.

At times you will need to euthanize dogs because of incurable medical or behavioral problems. Make sure all your volunteers are aware of your rescue's euthanasia policies and that they respect the reasons behind them. Otherwise, you may encounter resistance to your decisions and volunteer dissonance. Euthanasia is an emotional situation that must be handled delicately.

Do:

- DO clarify your rescue's policies on dogs with incurable illnesses and challenging behavioral issues.

- DO partner with several local vets and put together a spreadsheet of potential costs to treat different health issues.

- DO show respect and appreciation for your veterinary partners.

- DO be prepared for different medical issues by keeping certain medicines in stock for foster families to use.

- DO have a clear written policy for veterinary emergencies.

- DO develop a reference document for foster families on various medical concerns.

Don't:

- DON'T wait until the last minute to select a veterinary clinic or clinics.

- DON'T let foster dogs with contagious diseases affect other animals and people.

- DON'T let any of your foster dogs go without a collar and identification tags.

- DON'T spend thousands of dollars rehabilitating a dog with a bleak prognosis when there are many other more adoptable animals you could use that money to help.

Resources:

Rescuers Ring In (Veterinary Care): http://upforpups.org/2011/03/best-practices-veterinary-care/

Rescuers Ring In (Part 2): http://upforpups.org/2011/04/best-practices-standards-of-care/

Daddy's Emergency Animal Rescue Fund: http://www.millanfoundation.org/donate/dear.php

Discount vaccines and pet supplies: http://JeffersPet.com

Low Cost Spay/Neuter Clinics: http://neuterspay.org/ or http://www.aspca.org/pet-care/spayneuter/

Pet Health Care Gazette: http://www.pet-health-care-gazette.com/

Speaking for Spot: http://speakingforspot.com/blog/

Chapter 7:
Fundraising and Donations

Raising money for a non-profit dog rescue is an endless task, but don't be afraid to reach out, get creative, and have fun! Opportunities are endless if you can muster the manpower to manage money-generating events and activities. Having an organized, resourceful, outgoing events coordinator is important, and utilizing Facebook, Twitter, etc. and online newsletters can help you reach large groups efficiently. Some rescue even put together a fundraising committee. Each fundraising activity you attempt should have a goal, and each year you should reflect on those goals to evaluate which activities are most effective for your rescue.

Fundraising Ideas

There are many ways to raise money for your non-profit. In addition to developing your own fundraising initiatives, watch newspaper listings and listen for event notifications on the radio and on the television to find community events to participate in. Also keep an eye out for local businesses that are willing to fundraise for you. Sharing ideas and events with other related organizations can also be very helpful, but only plan events that you know you have the volunteer capacity to manage.

The following is a list of ideas that may help you to fundraise:

- **Soliciting donations**
    o Direct mail requests traditionally are the most successful for non-profits.
        - Send to previous adopters, local dog-friendly businesses, veterinary clinics, etc.
        - You can also request donations via email and social media (Facebook, Twitter, etc., but returns are usually limited compared with direct mail)

- o Post flyers about your need for donations at dog parks, dog daycares, vets, pet supply stores, and other dog-related businesses.

- o Get a weekly or monthly spot on a local television or radio program to advertise your adoptables and to recruit donors.

- o Make sure donating is easy for donors, whether they prefer to donate by check, online payment, or by credit card.

- o Place a donation jar on your table whenever your rescue participates at events.
  - Place a few dollars in the jar so people get the idea.

- o Post a highly-visible "donate" link on your website.

- o Be creative with your requests for donations.
  - Set up the choice on your website for automatic, reoccurring donations.
  - Allow "In honor of" or "In memory of" donations.
  - Give choices for donations for a specific animal's life-saving procedure, birthday, special event such as graduating from obedience school, etc.

- o Never say no to a donation of any kind.
  - If you get a donation of some item you don't need, donate it to another rescue or raffle it off.

- **Raffles**
  - o Offer a monthly item or basket that you advertise in your newsletter.
  - o Have a specialty raffle that you sell tickets for over a longer period of time.
    - E.g., raffle off a vacation over a two-month period.

- o Raffle a basket off at events you attend as a participant.
  - Have the item, a sign for your rescue, and raffle tickets available for purchase at events.
- o Note that to be legal, many states require special gambling licenses for raffling. Rescues seem to be able to circumnavigate this by calling it a "drawing." Check with your lawyer to find out your state's laws.

- **Events**
  - o Annual rescue "birthday party" or picnic is a win-win for everyone.
    - Fundraising avenues during these events include: raffles, games, registration fees, food, fashion show, vendor donations.
  - o Event ideas: walks (5Ks), meet-ups, dog washes, garage sales, trivia nights, bowling, bingo, wine and paint classes, neighborhood BBQs, etc.

- **Product sales**
  - o Bake sales, butter braids (pretzel twists), cookie dough sales, CandleLite, Scentsy, Avon, Yankee Candle, Pampered Chef, HappyTailsBooks.com, HelpingUdders.com, magazines, jewelry, etc.
  - o Sell rescue logo t-shirts online at and events.
  - o Have a dog/cat photo shoot or sell items with generic dog/cat photos, pet silhouettes, and paw prints; they appeal to a broad audience.
  - o Be careful not to overspend by ordering too many of the items you are selling. Pre-sales allow you to generate income before you order the items so you only order the amount you need.

- **Local business partnerships**
  - Leave a donation jar for your rescue at local businesses. (Don't forget to collect it!)
  - Ask a local business to host an event for you or to fundraise for you at an upcoming event of theirs.
  - Corporate matching programs
    - Many large corporations offer matching contributions for donations to 501(c)3 non-profits.
  - Ask for gift cards or items to raffle off.

- **Grants**
  - Look online or check with your town library to learn what grants are available and where to apply for them.

- **Do a Google search on "Animal Grants."**
  - PetCo, PetSmart, Target, Pet Supplies Plus, Rally to Rescue, and other organizations offer these types of grants.
    - Many grants require the applicant organization to be a 501(c)3 organization.
  - Designate a detail-oriented volunteer to research grants and fill out forms.
  - Pay attention to deadlines; these are very important.

- **Holiday opportunities**
  - Offer free gift wrapping labor to bookstores or department stores and put out a donation jar to get donations for the gift wrapping. Ask if the store will donate the gift wrapping paper, Scotch tape, and scissors, so your rescue doesn't have any expenses.

Donated Items

There is also great value in taking in donated items such as food, beds, leashes, collars, and other items foster parents might need. Previous adopters are a great resource for gently-used items, and local retail stores may be willing to partner with you to donate food and unused items such as their overstock or broken bags of dog food. Taking in used cars is very popular. Some people with timeshares are willing to donate a week in their condo for a rescue raffle prize (or for a reward for an outstanding volunteer), and some travel organizations are able to donate a free trip.

Do:

- DO be creative in coming up with ways to raise money for your rescue.

- DO try out time-tested ideas first.

- DO utilize easy ways to raise money, such as placing rescue jars in local businesses.

- DO make sure your rescue can handle whatever fundraising project you decide to take on.

- DO establish a fundraising committee for your rescue and let the members delegate assignments.

- DO assess your fundraising efforts annually to determine which are worth continuing.

Don't:

- DON'T plan fundraisers that require more work than your volunteers can handle.

- DON'T continue to rely on the same ways to raise money if they aren't effective for your rescue.

- DON'T be afraid to reach out to local businesses.

- DON'T say no to new fundraising ideas.

- DON'T use fundraising ideas that put your rescue at significant financial risk.

Resources:

Rescuers Ring In: http://upforpups.org/2011/04/best-practices-raising-money/

Daffron, Susan. 2009. Funds to the Rescue. http://www.amazon.com/Funds-Rescue-Fundraising-Humane-Animal/dp/0974924598

eHow Fundraising Ideas: http://www.ehow.com/list_5911968_fundraising-ideas-rescue-dogs.html

Fundraising tips for rescues: http://www.animalsheltertips.com/fundraising_events.html

Yankee Candle Fundraising: http://www.yankeecandlefundraising.com/

Chapter 8:
Managing Costs and Time

> "I would warn against credit of any kind, especially at start up. I only say this because I know how hard the first years were, and we only succeeded by staying out of debt. When we came across a situation that required more money than we had available, we created a fundraiser for that situation." –*Sharon Sleighter, Legacy Boxer Rescue*

Cost Management

Debt is the number one downfall of startup rescues. Debt is *not* your friend. Managing the costs involved in running a rescue is a daily task, and regular fundraising activities are at the center of your success because adoption fees are not going to cover the expenses of preparing dogs for forever homes (see *Chapter 7: Fundraising and Donations for fundraising ideas*). Rescues cannot exist on adoption fees alone. Some rescues do use credit cards when they feel they are absolutely at the end of their bank account, but this is generally not recommended. Raising money through fundraising activities is a much better choice because credit use is a slippery slope from which it can be difficult, if not impossible, to recover.

If you have a proven history of paying off credit cards in full each month, an alternative perspective is to use the same credit card for everything so that you can accrue points and get cash back. At no time should you allow a balance to linger on your rescue's card if you decide to take advantage of the perks of using a credit card. Again, for most people, credit is more dangerous than it is helpful.

Financial planning is an important part of a rescue's survival. Running a rescue is no different than running a business: it requires financial projections at the very least, so you know how much fundraising you need to do. Developing relationships with similar rescue organizations around the country can be especially valuable because they can help guide your financial projections.

In addition to fundraising, you should always have an eye on reducing costs. Can you negotiate better prices with your veterinary partners or other veterinarians in your area? Is there an emergency veterinarian who will extend discounted pricing to you? Can you buy food, toys, and other supplies in bulk (e.g., at Costco or online) at a discount? Can you reuse identification tags?

With regard to veterinary care, don't go overboard. Though all dogs should be vaccinated, spayed/neutered, and treated for any known health issue while in your care, you can leave "elective" vaccines up to the adopters to discuss with their veterinarians (see *Chapter 6: Veterinary Care* for a detailed discussion of veterinary care). Veterinary services must be paid in full at the time of service or on a monthly billing cycle. One strategy is to have your veterinarian keep a debit card on file to use for services as they are rendered. Regularly paying your veterinarians on their terms strengthens your relationship with them and provides you with a great reference for working with new vets in your area.

Time Management

Rescue administrators must become masters of time management, especially those who maintain regular jobs (almost everyone) and/or have families to care for in addition to their rescue activities. You must allocate time for the activities you can handle and delegate those you cannot. Do not let important activities such as fundraising slide by the wayside because you'd prefer to interact with dogs instead of people. Your rescue will not survive without a focus on these important tasks. Having said that, your mental health is also an important ingredient to success, and you must allocate time for yourself, your family, and your own animals.

There is a never-ending list of work to do in rescue. Know up front how much time you can commit on a daily basis. Try to set limits on how much time you are willing to spend working on your rescue each day, and stick to them. There are things you can do to work more efficiently, like committing yourself to being organized, keeping a separate email account for rescue business, and having a clear idea of your repetitive daily rescue tasks. You might want to get a laptop or smartphone to stay on top of your rescue emails, social media efforts, and adoption listings (see *Chapter 9: Marketing*).

Web-based computer programs like Dropbox or Google Docs can help rescue volunteers quickly access documents without constantly having to call board members about them. You can upload your files to these hosts and share specific folders with volunteers. This is also helpful in the unfortunate circumstance that your computer crashes because your documents will be hosted online. Many of these types of programs are free.

Retrieving multiple voicemail messages can be very time consuming, but it also can be easily delegated to volunteers. Rescuegroups.org offers a voicemail package that allows you to set up multiple mailboxes on a single phone number. You can set your voicemail with menu options so that message will be distributed to the appropriate volunteer.

Networking

Networking with other rescuers can significantly help you manage your time and your sanity. You'll find many others who share your love of dogs and your passion for rescue at local adoption events. Additionally, online networking sites such as breed message boards and Facebook allow you to meet other like-minded people without having to leave the comfort of your own home. It's just plain fun to have friends who are also heavily involved in rescue, and sharing your burdens with them can help you to get through rescue challenges more efficiently. Even if you see yourself as more of a "dog person" than a "people person," do not discount the value of human empathy.

Do:

- DO be careful if your rescue decides to use a credit card. Only charge what can be paid off monthly.

- DO take financial planning seriously.

- DO consider ways to save your rescue and foster volunteers' money.

- DO delegate responsibilities so volunteers don't burn out and leave the rescue.

- DO make time for yourself and your family.

Don't:

- DON'T let the rescue go into debt.

- DON'T get behind in paying your rescue's veterinarian bills.

- DON'T let daily rescue tasks get waylaid.

- DON'T forget to ask for help when you need it.

Resources:

Rescuers Ring In:
http://upforpups.org/2011/04/best-practices-managing-costs/

Allen, David. 2002. Getting Things Done: The Art of Stress-Free Productivity. http://www.amazon.com/Getting-Things-Done-Stress-Free-Productivity/dp/0142000280/ref=sr_1_3?ie=UTF8&qid=1305236691&sr=8-3

Dropbox: http://dropbox.com

Google Docs: http://docs.google.com

Jeffers Pet: http://JeffersPet.com

Ketchum Manufacturing discounted pet tags:
http://www.ketchummfg.com/c8/Bone-110-c51.html

Rescuegroups.org: http://rescuegroups.org

Chapter 9:
Marketing

Marketing is vital to a rescue's success. Attending events, developing a good website, and posting your adoptable pets with online listing services are a good start, but it's just that: a start. You must continuously reach out to potential volunteers and adopters, or you will eventually find yourself caring for a lot of dogs alone.

Keep in mind that marketing is different from fundraising. While fundraising is a way of raising funds for your rescue so you can buy what is needed for the foster dogs, marketing is the means by which you *introduce* people to your rescue and your adoptable pets. No matter how noble a rescue's intentions, without effective marketing, that rescue's lifespan will be cut short.

This chapter provides you with several ideas and resources for successful marketing. It is broken down into three main sections: Marketing Avenues, Great Websites, and Indispensible Tips for Marketing Adoptable Dogs.

Marketing Avenues

Blogs: Blogs can take a long time to gain a fan base, but they're a great way to call attention to important topics you'd like to discuss and to ensure your website is constantly receiving new content. Http://Wordpress.com and http://Blogger.com are two popular blog-hosting services that allow you to have a stand-alone blog (good) or a blog embedded in your website (better). There are many different things you can do with a blog, like sharing foster parent experiences, videos of adoptable dogs, and information about the breed. Blogs are also a good forum for discussing animal advocacy topics. The wonderful thing about blogs is that people can leave comments, which can lead to some very thoughtful discussions and higher search engine rankings.

Contests: Winning contests, like local "hometown hero" contests, is a great way to get publicity for your organization. It may seem crazy to nominate yourself, but hey, you're doing a good job, and people need to know about it!

Local businesses: Have local businesses keep literature about your rescue in their checkout areas or post signs in their windows. As discussed in *Chapter 7: Fundraising and Donations,* you could even ask them to put a jar out for people's spare change. In this case, make sure that your jar clearly states your website and that you have dogs available for adoption. Some local businesses have heavily-trafficked websites, too. You might ask them to post a badge (small image that links to your website) on their website. Do the same for them.

Don't forget that your veterinarians are local businesses, too. They are a great place to post flyers and literature about your organization, and they may also be willing to post information about your organization on their websites. Not only does advertising your organization on veterinary websites help you adopt out more dogs, but it helps the veterinary office to look good in the eyes of the community in that it supports rescue.

Local events: Local events, both pet- and community-related, enable rescues to get themselves out in front of potential volunteers and adopters. These events include local fairs, pet supply store adoption events, holiday functions, parades, etc. If you just started your rescue, you'll need to attend all of these events, but as your volunteer base grows, you can often find other enthusiastic pet lovers to represent your organization. Many rescues rely heavily on local events when they are just getting started, but sometimes, as their reputations grow, they are able to pick and choose which events they want to attend and focus more on their web presence.

Local media: Keep a list of local media contacts on hand and write or call them periodically when an extraordinary animal comes across your path. Giving your media contacts useful leads is always appreciated and can get you a foot in the door for when you need publicity. Remember to get a list of deadlines for your media contacts and give them information far enough in advance, so they can publicize an event or to get an article in the media.

Newsletters: Many rescues see newsletters as their most valuable fundraising tools. Almost every rescue sends email newsletters, although a few still send a quarterly or annual snail mail newsletter, too. Do not *send* email newsletters from your personal email address. As your mailing list grows, your server will shut you down for "spamming." A much better idea is to use a service such as Vertical Response, which offers great non-profit discounts (and freebies) and also allows you to track important data such as opens and *click-throughs*. Make sure the people you are mailing to have opted-in (requested to receive your newsletter), or you will be in violation of anti-spamming laws.

Great newsletters include more than just calls to action, although it is perfectly acceptable to list your volunteer and donation needs in your newsletter. Here are some other items to include:

- Interesting facts, stories, or quotes: Have you come across anything dog-related lately that made you laugh, cry, or think? Your readers probably want to know about it, too.

- Statistics: How many pets have you saved this year? How much have you spent? What are your goals?

- Veterinary tips: Giving a local veterinarian a column in your newsletter is great marketing for the vet and good for you, too. The vet can address common issues of which your readers should be aware.

- Events: Are there dog-friendly events coming up in your region? Are you hosting any events? Attending any adoption fairs?

- Alumni "happy tails": Everyone loves a success story.

- Pet of the month: Is there an adoptable pet who has been overlooked? Here is your change to highlight him or her.

- Merchandise: Are you selling any breed-specific or rescue-specific merchandise?

- Volunteer spotlight: A great place to honor volunteers.

- Humane education: Puppy mills, dog fighting, no-choke collar campaigns, dog training, etc. What can you include in your newsletter that will help readers become more knowledgeable about animal welfare issues?

- Volunteer opportunities: How can people help you? What are your rescue's immediate needs?

- Donations: How can people make donations to you? Are there donors you want to thank (be sure these people want their names disclosed before publishing them)?

Pet adoption sites: Most pet adoption sites do not charge rescues for listing their adoptables, and they are a great way to get your adoptables out in front of people because they usually have good search engine optimization (ranking), which puts them at the top of people's web searches. RescueGroups.org is one website that allows rescues to update their adoptable dogs on many different adoption websites at once. They also offer several other rescue management tools.

Petfinder.com is by far the largest adoption website, but other websites like Adoptapet.com are also worth your time.

Paid Advertising: Some rescues use paid advertising offered by businesses like Google AdWords or Facebook Advertising. With both of these advertising vehicles, you can declare exactly how much you want to spend per day so that you don't go over your predetermined budget, and you can identify the types of individuals you'd like to have view your ads via keywords (words that you think interested adopters would search). Sign up with these businesses to receive their alerts or newsletters, and you'll receive offers for some free advertising, too.

Social media networking: "Social media networking" means using websites such as Twitter, Facebook, Dogster, and message boards to connect with like-minded people. These websites generally don't charge for use and can provide you access to myriad people who otherwise may not find your rescue. The real expense in using these resources is time, so help yourself by finding a reliable, articulate volunteer to manage your social media networking.

Most rescues have Facebook fan pages that allow you to constantly update your "fans" with your activities. There are instructions online for how to set up a Facebook fan page. Here are some tips for Facebooking success:

- Post often and regularly.

- Do not ask for something in every post.

    o Keep donation requests to a minimum so that when you really need money, people will take note. If you're constantly asking people to donate, you will lose fans.

- Get to know your fans.

    o Answer their questions and engage them.

    o Have them post themed pictures of their pets during major holidays and then choose one every day as your profile picture of the day.

    Poll your fans. (E.g., ask your fans how they deal with a particular behavioral and/or health issue.)

- Post helpful health and training tips for your rescue's specific breed or for dogs in general.

- Do not continuously post about how sick your incoming dogs are.

    o People don't want to be depressed every time they visit your page.

    o Post quotes, links to funny videos, and other uplifting things.

- Add a "donate" tab to your Facebook page using static FBML.

- Have fun!

Youtube: As of the publication of this manual, http://youtube. com is the second most heavily-trafficked search engine in the world. Making a video of your adopted dogs is a great way to generate interest in your rescue. Having a local artist compose music for your video is awesome, but if you don't have those kinds of resources, there are many websites offering royalty-free music for you to use and Youtube offers a music drop-in option now, too (Youtube will remove your music if they feel it infringes on a copyright). Make sure to include your web address and your organization's mission in the description section when you post your video.

> Ask your foster families to film their foster dogs and upload the videos to Youtube. Many listing services allow you to post Youtube-hosted videos now, and it is also very easy to embed these videos on your own website.

> Check out http://www.OneTrueMedia.com for help making a video or photo montage. Alternatively, you can find free, easy-to-use movie-making software downloads online like Windows Movie Maker.

Great Websites

A rescue organization should have a website that is either named after the organization (ex. http://www.bostonbrigade.com/) or easy to remember (e.g., http://www.savetheboxers.com/). If your name is very long, you might consider an abbreviation (e.g., http://www. brood-va.org/). If you think of several good web names that aren't already taken, you can purchase them inexpensively and simply point them to your main domain name using your hosting service's control panel. Organizations like Petfinder.com offer free websites with limited functionality, which can be a good starting point for new rescue organizations. Most rescues then look for something more robust, but even extremely versatile websites don't need to cost more than $5-$7 per month plus $10 per year for the domain name.

User-friendly web development platforms that do not require the web-builder to have an in-depth knowledge of html are readily available. One very popular platform is http://Wordpress.com. This platform can be installed via a hosting service and offers "plugins," easy-to-configure functionalities like contact forms, broken link checkers, and spam filters.

Website Design: When planning your website, the first thing to consider is why people will visit your website. Since a good website is the single most important marketing tool for a growing rescue organization, it is important to spend some time and thought planning it. Unfortunately, many rescues do not bother to carefully consider website features that may turn off visitors. Some *undesirable* website features include:

- Music and flashy content
    - o Just think about a person opening your website while at work… Awkward!
- Too many buttons/choices
- Difficult to locate key pages (adoptable pets, donations, volunteers, events)
- Patterned background behind text
    - o Difficult to read
- Many different fonts and font sizes

A good website takes into account the visitor's purpose(s) and fulfills them easily. For the most part, people visit rescue websites for a few specific reasons:

- To adopt a pet
- To learn about the organization (and the breed, for breed-specific rescues)
- To make a donation
- To volunteer
- To find out about upcoming events

Rescue websites should direct visitors easily to these key items. Organize links across the top of the page with related sub-links that appear when someone rolls his or her cursor over the main header. Organizing these key links on the left-hand side of the page is also acceptable. Identify pages by standard key terms. For example, "Adoptable Dogs" is a much better link name than "Furries Seeking Furevers." People are at your site for a purpose, and if that purpose isn't fulfilled quickly, they will move on.

Many people visit rescue websites because they want to make donations. Make the donate button visible on every page and be sure it  clearly says, "Donate." Payment processing services like Paypal have a standard button that many non-profits use. It's easily recognizable.

Pages: Most websites include the following pages on their websites. Note that the pages are listed under the exact names listed below. (E.g., "About" is always the name of the background information page of a website. Straying from the term "About" causes confusion more than it expresses individuality.)

About: The about page is usually the first link on the navigation bar (the vertical or horizontal main menu). This page succinctly describes the rescue's mission, the geographical area it serves, key points of success, and information about the founders. Often rescues will include a story of the animal who inspired the rescuer(s) to found the rescue. Photos of the founding pets and people are always a good idea. If you are a 501(c)3 non-profit, list this fact on the "About" page and in the website footer (the information at the bottom of the website that appears on every page).

Adoptable Dogs: There are different schools of thought on how to organize the Adoptable Dogs page. Some rescues have this link direct people first to a list of their adoption rules. Other rescues have this link take potential adopters directly to a listing of adoptable dogs. The authors of this manual feel that the best thing to do is to have this link take visitors directly to photos and write-ups of adoptable dogs because your website should make learning about your rescue and finding adoptable dogs easy. There is plenty of time to drop the hammer about adoption rules during the application process, but at this point, the visitor is just interested in seeing what dogs you have available.

Using a listing service like Petfinder.com is a great idea because these listing websites much higher on search engines than most rescues and can help potential adopters find your rescue. Additionally, the listing websites generally have listing tools that anyone can use, whereas if you list your adoptable dogs through your own website, you need a qualified webmaster to change the listings every time a dog is adopted or your rescue gets in a new foster dog. Most pet listing websites have a way to embed your listing within your website while still updating them through their user-friendly interface. If this all sounds like gobbledegoo to you, then let's just say you should definitely use a listing service.

Your Adoptable Dogs link can have several sub-menus. For example, you may have separate pages for adoption requirements, breed information, and the adoption application.

Volunteer: Your website should convey the idea that volunteering with your rescue is easy, fun, and rewarding. List as wide a breadth of volunteer opportunities as possible so that potential volunteers can see all of the different ways they can help your organization. Include a link to your foster application, which ideally is a form on your website that is easily submitted with the click of a button. You can update this page regularly to reflect your current volunteer needs.

Donate: Do *not* list 500 different ways for people to donate, and do *not* hide this page under a different main menu listing. If someone is coming to your website to donate to your rescue, make it easy for them! Have a donate button on your home page and a donation page with further options and an address to which people can mail checks. Many rescues use this page to list two different donate options: One-time and Recurring. It's also a good idea to list how different donation amounts will help your rescue. For example: $25 buys annual vaccines for one dog, $85 buys one neuter, $350 buys a cherry eye surgery, etc.

There are many different services that will process payments for your rescue. http://Paypal.com, http://Amazon.com, and http://Justgive.org have no annual fee for their basic service. Instead, they take a reasonable percentage and/or a small flat fee from each donation. Buying your own credit card processing service is usually more costly, but not offering some kind of credit card processing service will result in diminished donations.

Events: This page should list any adoption and fundraising events at which your rescue will be present. Google Calendars allow you to embed your calendar in your website, which makes for easy updates. Also, all volunteers to whom you give permission can access these calendars. At the very least, simply list the places, dates, and times on your website for where and when you will have representatives available.

Contact: This is usually the rightmost link on the navigation bar. The page should include an email address, phone number, and a physical address, at the minimum. Some rescues list several different contact people for different purposes, which is fine so long as the list doesn't exceed five people or so and a "general inquiries" contact is also listed. Make sure your representatives respond to all inquiries *within 24 hours.*

Other pages: Some rescues list a Buy or Marketplace page if they sell things to help with fundraising. Check into local and federal regulations about whether you need a retail license to sell items on your website. Other popular pages include a resource page where people can find additional information and an alumni page where people can read "happy tails" about successful adoptions (usually a sub-menu under Adoptable Dogs).

The purpose of using these easily recognizable names for your navigation links is not to stifle creativity but instead to make it easy for visitors to move around your website. A well-organized website featuring concise, useful content and colorful photos and videos related to your rescue's mission will set your organization apart. Additionally, having a well-designed website will help you to run your rescue more efficiently because potential volunteers and adopters will be able to find the information they are seeking *on your website,* resulting in less unnecessary communications for you.

Easily navigable rescue websites are, unfortunately, in short supply. Here are some rescue websites that break the mold:

- http://www.brood-va.org/
- http://www.bostonbrigade.com/
- http://www.chihuahuarescueofsandiego.com/
- http://www.dogsforthedeaf.org/
- http://www.pugpartners.com/

Site maintenance: Someone should check your rescue's websites regularly for broken links. There is software available to do this for you, or hiring your friend's computer-savvy 10-year-old works. Websites should also be regularly reviewed for outdated information, and content should be updated as frequently as possible because search engines like keyword-heavy websites that are frequently updated with new content. Google AdWords can help you to find out the keywords you should include most frequently on your website, as this will help you to rise in search engine rankings (You can also advertise your site using AdWords, but it is not free).

The most important take away from this section is that visitors will be most likely to find you and have success with your website if it is up-to-date, easy to navigate, and concise, so do your best to accommodate them by thoughtfully planning your website.

Indispensible Tips for Marketing Adoptable Dogs

Whether you are marketing your adoptable dogs through posters hung at coffee shops, adoption websites, your website, or other print media, having eye-catching photos and an honest yet compelling biography of each foster dog is essential.

Photos: Photos are the first thing potential adopters notice, and if you do a good job, the pictures will tug on their heartstrings.

Which dog would you adopt?

The above photo shows a grumpy-looking Boxer who looks unsure of the photographer and a happy-looking Boxer who might like to go for a swim. If a person is thinking of adopting a companion to spend his or her life with, consciously or subconsciously he or she is probably going to be more attracted to the dog who looks like fun. Photos are a great way to show off a dog's personality and the value he or she will provide to a new family. They are usually the first piece of information a potential adopter gets about a dog aside from the dog's name, so it's important they are done well.

Do not expect your foster parents to know how to take good photos. You can help them by supplying some photo guidelines and expectations in your initial fostering paperwork. Here are some tips you might include:

- Photograph dogs outside. If it's very bright outside, have the animal sit or lie down in the shade. If the dog is too hyper, let him or her run around for a while, and then try again. If that doesn't work, try having the dog sit in a car.

- Photograph the dog in front of a background against which he or she stands out. (E.g., don't photograph a black dog sitting on a black chair.)

- Squeeze a squeaky toy behind your back or over the dog's head to grab his or her attention. Talking sweetly or excitedly can help make the dog perk up his or her ears, too.

- Take your time. Snap a few photos here and there. You never know what you may get.

- Try to take photos that capture the dog's personality. If he or she loves toys, take pictures of him or her playing with them. If the dog has a wonderful breed characteristic, highlight that in the photos. Accentuate the positive and downplay the negative.

- Avoid using a flash. Dogs with glowing eyes may send the wrong message!

- Hold the camera still, and if the photos come out blurry, try again.

Examples:

Wish you were here!

Cheeseburger!

Wanna play?

As you can see, the photos don't have to be perfect. They simply need to express the dog's personality and entice the reader to want to learn more.

Videos: Many adoption websites allow you to post videos of your adoptable dogs, and you can certainly post videos on your own website. While good photos are absolutely essential, videos can be very helpful, especially for marketing dogs who are aged or have disabilities. If you can show a potential adopter that a dog still has some fun left in him or her or that managing a disability is not that big a deal, it can help break down barriers and encourage adopters to give a dog they might otherwise overlook a chance.

Descriptions: After a potential adopter falls in love with a photo, the interested person's next step is to read the bio. If the bio gruffly lists only the dog's age, weight, and sex, people are likely to move on. Instead, think about the perfect person for your adoptable dog and write a compelling bio to draw that person in. A good bio is honest about a dog's "issues" but tends to dwell more on the positive than the negative. It can be written from the dog's perspective or from a human perspective.

Example:

Last month was very special for me. After five years of sitting in a wire cage, I finally got to touch grass for the first time! Nobody ever talked to me at the place where I lived, but when I came to my foster home, I got a name: Ruby. Doesn't that have a nice ring? It feels so good to run around the yard and hear people calling my name. Sometimes I'm so happy that I run up to them and stretch my paws up to the sky! They tell me I shouldn't do that so much, but hey, I only weigh 20 pounds, and I'm just looking for a hug! I guess I'll work on it. But really, I'm just so happy to hang out with my people and cuddle. I like other dogs and cats, too, but they don't feed me cheese, so I'll take people first any day. I went to a veterinarian recently, and he poked at me. The good news is I heard I don't have to go back for another year. I had a lot to learn about living in a house when I came to my foster home, but my foster mom says I'm catching on fast. I still have a few accidents here and there, but I know I'll get this potty training thing down in no time. I'm pretty easy to care for. I know how to entertain myself when my foster parents aren't home, but I do like to go for our morning and evening walks. Would you like to take a walk with me?

Do:

- DO make a marketing plan and set aside time for marketing activities.

- DO establish a marketing committee for your rescue.

- DO delegate specific marketing tasks to volunteers according to their strengths.

- DO take the advice listed herein about website design.

- DO include information about taking photos and videos in your foster manual.

- DO have a donation link on your homepage.

Don't:

- DON'T leave marketing tasks unassigned.

- DON'T take longer than 24 hours to respond to email and phone inquiries.

- DON'T leave out-of-date information and broken links on your website.

- DON'T make your website difficult for a visitor to use.

- DON'T make music play automatically on your website, no matter how much you like that song. You can always include a link for people to click on if they'd like to hear it.

Resources:

Rescuers Ring In:
http://upforpups.org/2011/04/best-practices-marketing/

Anti-spamming laws: http://business.ftc.gov/documents/bus61-can-spam-act-compliance-guide-business

Broken link checker software: http://linkchecker.sourceforge.net/

Facebook advertising: http://www.facebook.com/advertising/

Google

    AdWords: https://adwords.google.com/

    Calendar: https://www.google.com/calendar/

Movie-making tools

    One True Media: http://onetruemedia.com

    Windows Live Movie Maker: http://explore.live.com/windows-live-movie-maker?os=other

Newsletter tools

    Constant Contact: http://constantcontact.com

    Vertical Response: http://verticalresponse.com

Social media tools

    Facebook page setup:
    http://www.facebook.com/pages/create.php

    Static FBML how-to (for adding a "donate" tab to your FB page): http://www.socialmediaexaminer.com/how-to-customize-your-facebook-page-using-static-fbml/

    Twitter: http://twitter.com

    Youtube: http://youtube.com

Listing help

    Adopt a Pet: http://www.adoptapet.com/

    Petfinder.com: http://petfinder.com

    Rescue listing support service: http://rescuegroups.org

Web/blog hosting

    Blogger: http://blogger.com

    Hostmonster: http://hostmonster.com

    GoDaddy: http://godaddy.com

    Wordpress: http://wordpress.org

Chapter 10:
Volunteers

Volunteers give their time and resources for free, a fact that must be recognized and respected. They come in all shapes and sizes, from children to the elderly, and they serve as the backbone to a rescue's success. Most rescues do not have any paid positions and survive solely on the goodwill and efforts of volunteers.

Building a good volunteer base takes time and planning. The first step in planning is to identify your needs. Assess your own strengths and weaknesses, identify the items you like to do, and recognize the tasks that will burn you out quickly. Then, identify what kind of volunteers can bring strengths to fill in for your weaknesses, can handle the things you don't have time for, and can do the things that will burn you out. Write volunteer job descriptions and post them on the website for people to see, but also leave the door open for people to come to you with ideas on how they would like to volunteer with your organization. Not everyone fits into a box, but he or she may bring something new to the table that you didn't even know you needed help with. If possible, do not turn people down when they offer to volunteer. Plan ahead for roles that can be filled by "less desirable" volunteers. For example, perhaps they can go through your website and make sure none of the links are broken, or they can check the dog descriptions weekly for typos. Even if you have misgivings about working with them, find them some small role they can fill. You never know when you'll wish you had them, and you don't want people badmouthing your rescue that they offered to help and you denied them the opportunity or didn't get back to them. Strive to match volunteer abilities with specific tasks they will enjoy and complete successfully.

Where to Find Volunteers

Attract volunteers through online advertising via your website, Facebook, Twitter, message boards, etc. Find them at local events like adoption days and community fairs. Post flyers at coffee shops, pet supply stores, groomers, veterinary offices, and other local businesses. Current volunteers and people who have had a good experience adopting from you are a great source of new volunteers. You can reach out to these people by including information about volunteering in your adoption kits and making sure to have brochures or postcards about volunteering available at every event you attend. Have a link on your website's navigation bar that says, "Volunteer" and leads to a page with clear information about how to volunteer with your rescue and what volunteering entails.

Local corporations also are a good resource for volunteers. Most big corporations have employee newsletters or message boards where they might advertise your volunteering needs for free. Some give employees additional benefits for volunteer work. You may also tap into local schools, churches, various social and charity clubs such as Optimist clubs and scout troops.

Most rescues make a volunteer application available online, which may include a non-disclosure agreement and/or liability waiver. Consult a lawyer about these items. The application can be a web form or something people can download, print, fill out, and return. Either way, it should include questions that  help your volunteer coordinator understand the volunteer applicant's strengths, expectations, interests, and availability. The application should also include the person's contact information and information about current pets and family, if he or she wishes to foster. (Your rescue may wish to have a separate foster home application.)

Your website should state how long it takes you to get back to potential volunteers, and you should absolutely get back to them within that time frame, whether you currently have a need for that volunteer or not. Have a knowledgeable volunteer coordinator contact the new volunteer to discuss the volunteer "job" description, expectations, and responsibilities. The coordinator should anticipate questions about the rescue and know how to get answers to questions he or she may not be able to answer immediately. The coordinator should also follow up with the volunteer after the volunteer's first rescue experience in order thank the volunteer, answer questions, and give feedback. Thank-you notes are always a nice touch.

Maintaining Volunteers

Volunteers expect trust, respect, communication, and empowerment. It is not uncommon for a rescue founder to try to control everything in his or her rescue because, well, founding a rescue generally takes a commanding personality. Sometimes rescue founders try to do everything themselves because they feel like no one else can do anything as good as they can, but these rescuers quickly find themselves with a significant volunteer turnover issue. A true leader, one who runs a successful rescue with happy, long-lasting volunteers, funnels that controlling need into a way of gently guiding his or her organization—giving volunteers the tools they need to be successful—and then letting them work their magic. These leaders have discovered that sometimes volunteers can do things even better than they can. Volunteers bring new ideas, new energy, and a new network of potential supporters.

As rescues grow, so does the need to delegate tasks. Volunteer management is one of those tasks, and that role may be broken down further into the different types of volunteers and/or different regions. For example, an event coordinator may also manage event volunteers, and a foster coordinator may manage foster training and support as well as foster volunteer issues. For larger rescues, this may be broken down by state or by region. Volunteers should be provided with information about who they are to contact when they need something. Rescue founders and board members need to be accessible to volunteers as well, reminding volunteers that they are valuable members of the team and that their input is valued.

People in volunteer management positions need good "people skills." They need to communicate clearly, regularly, and effectively and make themselves available to volunteers when they are needed. For foster coordinators, this may mean taking phone calls in the middle of the night—foster dog emergencies can't wait, and a foster home with no support in an emergency will not remain a foster home for long.

Terminating Volunteers

If, at any time, it becomes obvious that the volunteer is not a good fit for the organization, the founders or board members need to politely terminate the volunteer. A passive-aggressive approach where the volunteer is ignored will create hard feelings just as much as a harsh termination will, so have a volunteer termination procedure laid out beforehand, and stick to it. Include information about termination in the volunteer welcome packet to ensure volunteers clearly understand expectations. If you do terminate a volunteer, give the person a reason and wish that person well. Do not "blame" anyone. State it in terms of organizational needs and the volunteer's best interest.

Communication with Volunteers

Rescues use many different means to communicate with their volunteers. Some do a monthly newsletter just for volunteers; others use Yahoo Groups, Twitter, Facebook, or other social media networking tools. Websites like Dropbox or Google Docs allow you to post documents online for multiple people to access and edit, which can be helpful in communicating with volunteers.

Example Volunteer Positions

Below are several ideas of volunteer positions you may want to fill for your rescue. However, remember that volunteers exist to facilitate adoptions, not to add more bureaucracy. Before creating a position, ask yourself how it will truly help you to adopt out more dogs to good homes. If you can't answer that question, you don't need the position. An alternative is to form committees to handle certain tasks, like marketing and fundraising, but the same rule about their usefulness to your ultimate goal applies. Many rescues have so many committees and volunteers involved in the adoption process that their adoption rate is lower and their return rate is higher than it would be were there less people involved in the process. Don't be that rescue.

- **Adoption coordinator:** Almost every rescue has someone who screens applicants. Some rescues then distribute applications to foster homes for the foster parents to choose a suitable adopter for their dogs,* while others feel this is better handled by a centralized committee. Whoever is in charge, dogs should not be adopted out without someone doing reference checks, a home visit, and an interview. Some rescues have foster parents coordinate and execute most of these tasks, while other rescues have specific volunteers that handle each one. Some related positions may include **home check coordinator, applicant interviewer, reference checker, adoption counselor** (generally responsible for follow-up after a dog is adopted), **and foster adoption liaison** (works with foster homes to help determine which dogs are best for which applicants).

- **Board of directors:** The size of a Board of Directors varies from rescue to rescue, but as a 501(c)3 non-profit, you are required by federal law to have at least three officers. Some rescues heavily utilize these officers, while others just put people in these positions as a matter of law. A rescue should at least have an advisory board that can help with major decisions. Some boards meet monthly, others quarterly, others annually. Rescues that are very spread out may need to meet virtually using a service like GoTo Meeting, Skype, or other remote meeting-facilitation programs. Officers should have term limits for two reasons: to keep new ideas coming in and to give you an easy out if a person isn't right for the position. The Board of Directors positions may include the Director, Treasurer, Secretary, and At-Large Members. Having an accountant or finance person in the treasurer position can be very helpful.

---

* Most experienced foster parents feel that the best practice is to let the foster homes choose the right adopter for their dogs because they know the dogs best and by eliminating extra people in the process, the dogs get adopted much more quickly.

- **Correspondence coordinator:** This may be a person or group of people who ensure that calls and emails are returned in a timely manner. If they are experienced volunteers, they may be able to answer many inquiries on their own, but they should also be knowledgeable enough about the organization to know how to delegate calls and emails.

- **Evaluators/trainers:** Some rescues have special volunteers with dog behavior or training backgrounds who can evaluate and help dogs with health and behavioral issues.

- **Event coordinator:** This person should be outgoing and organized, with a good knowledge of community events and adoption fair opportunities. He or she is usually responsible for organizing and staffing meet-and-greets and fundraising events. This position is usually separate from the Marketing Manager, but for smaller rescues, an events coordinator may also be responsible for marketing.

- **Event volunteers:** These people promote the rescue and adoptable dogs at events. They may or may not have other volunteer positions within the rescue, and they may be willing transport foster dogs to and from the events they attend. They should have a working knowledge of the rescue and the adoption process.

- **Foster home coordinator:** This volunteer makes regular phone calls to the foster families to offer support and solicit updates on foster dogs. He or she should be able to address any foster-related issues in a timely manner and is responsible for ensuring foster homes are provided with the appropriate paperwork, supplies (microchips, adoption kits, medicines, etc.), and whatever else they need.

- **Foster parents:** These are individuals/families who care for dogs in their homes until the appropriate forever home is identified. Fostering is discussed thoroughly in *Chapter 11: Foster Home Management.*

- **Grant-writing/fundraising volunteers:** Grant-writing requires attention to detail, resourcefulness, and time to find and fill out the forms completely. Fundraising volunteers may also be responsible for sending thank-you notes to donors, sending letters asking for donations, etc. as well as working with the Events Coordinator to plan fundraising events.

- **Intake coordinator:** This volunteer is responsible for the intake of dogs from shelters and families. This person may also handle dogs released from breeders, purchased at auctions, or otherwise surrendered from puppy mills, but that may require a separate volunteer. The intake coordinator maintains the flow of dogs to avoid overwhelming a rescue's resources and ensures they are placed in foster homes.

- **Marketing manager:** It is helpful for this person to have an understanding of graphic design in order to create advertisements, flyers, etc. This person is responsible for identifying and executing marketing opportunities and supporting the events coordinator with internal and external event promotion. This person may also be in charge of the rescue newsletter and website, although the Web Master may be a separate position.

- **Transport coordinator:** This position is responsible for arranging transport for dogs to and from the rescue organization, to veterinarian visits, and to events (when necessary). They work with organizations and individuals to ensure dogs can get the care they need and then ultimately find their way to their forever families.

- **Transport volunteers:** Transport volunteers help with any type of transport needed by the rescue. Some foster homes need help getting dogs to vet visits and events, while others can do it themselves. Some dogs come into rescue from far away and require a series of transport volunteers to get them from point "A" to point "B." A detailed discussion of transport is provided in *Chapter 13: Transporting Animals.*

- **Vet coordinator:** Some rescues have foster homes directly contact approved vets for their foster dogs' care, while others prefer to have a specific volunteer speak with vet offices to arrange appointments. This person may be responsible for distributing medications to foster families.

- Rescues with physical shelter facilities also need care and maintenance volunteers.

Committees:

Some rescues prefer to have committees instead of individual volunteer positions. Here are some examples; though having *all* of these committees usually causes more harm than good for an organization. Again, it is important to choose only the volunteer positions and committees that *facilitate* adoptions and to eliminate any committees or positions that cause the adoption process to move more inefficiently.

- **Management committee:** This committee consists of core volunteers who chair more specific committees and handle rescue decisions.

- **Foster committee:** The foster committee works closely with the intake committee to place needy dogs into foster care. They try to match up the best dog for the best foster home given the limited information a rescue generally receives about incoming dogs.

- **Intake committee:** The intake committee tracks and records needy dogs who fit the rescue's mission. They work to match these dogs up with foster homes and ask the appropriate volunteers to evaluate potential intakes. They are also responsible for maintaining contact with shelters, surrendering families, and breeders whose dogs need your help until foster care is available or the dog is safe via other avenues (reclaimed, adopted from the shelter, etc). Members of this committee work closely with the members of the foster committee to be sure they're aware of which dogs most urgently need to go to foster homes.

o **Evaluation volunteers:** If a rescue has a clearly-defined evaluation process, it can send volunteers to meet potential incoming dogs and evaluate them. A good rule of thumb is to make sure the volunteer has been active with the rescue for at least several months and has demonstrated an understanding of dog behavior. Reports from these volunteers are very helpful in placing needy dogs in appropriate foster homes.

- **Adoption applications committee:** This committee is responsible for the adoption application process and for communication with all applicants. Committee members take care of reference checks, landlord checks, veterinarian checks, home visits, and all correspondences with applicants. They assign adoption counselors to approved applicants.

  o **Adoption counselors:** All volunteers are eligible to serve as adoption counselors after they have been with the rescue long enough to "have a good grasp of the process." An adoption counselor acts in concert with foster parents to set up meetings with potential matches for their foster dogs. In many cases, foster parents serve as the adoption counselors and are given total power to place their foster dogs with approved applicants.* They know their dogs best, and they can best place that animal into a home that will fit his or her needs. Management only gets involved if there is an issue or concern.

- **Web committee:** This committee maintains the website and the rescue's online presence. Some rescues have an online volunteer portal (ex. Google Docs), which the web committee also maintains.

- **Veterinary committee:** This committee handles all issues related to veterinary care, including scheduling appointments and transportation (when necessary), and ensuring that foster homes have the necessary medications for their foster dogs.

- **Welcome committee:** This committee is responsible for new volunteer orientation. Committee members communicate with volunteers when they first begin helping the rescue to be sure they understand their tasks and to help them feel like part of the rescue team.

- Thank-you committee: Volunteers for this committee send thank you cards to all adopters and supporters (donations).

- Fundraising, marketing, and PR committee: These volunteers identify events to attend and then recruit volunteers to staff the events. They write press releases, take advantage of marketing opportunities, and write grants for the rescue.

When a rescue has official volunteer positions or committees, usually each position or committee is responsible for a unique voicemail box and email address. The person filling that position or one volunteer for each committee should be responsible for checking the voicemail/email and responding to inquiries within 24 hours.

Do:

- DO write job descriptions for all of your volunteer positions and post them on your website.

- DO have potential volunteers fill out applications that help you to fit their talents and desires with your rescue's needs.

- DO have regular meetings with all committees or key volunteers, whether via phone or in person.

- DO treat all volunteers with respect and kindness, even when you have to ask a volunteer to leave the rescue.

- DO develop creative means to attract volunteers.

- DO be sure your volunteers have all the information they need to best represent the rescue.

Don't:

- DON'T build committees and volunteer positions simply to create bureaucracy.

- DON'T send volunteers out unprepared.

- DON'T keep volunteers who aren't productive or working well with the rescue.

- DON'T give volunteers more than they can handle.

Resources:

Rescuers Ring In: http://upforpups.org/2011/04/best-practices-volunteers/

Online conferencing:

GoTo Meeting: http://gotomeeting.com

Skype: http://skype.com

Rescue voicemail and other needs: http://www.rescuegroups.org

Chapter 11:
Foster Home Management

Most rescues cannot exist without a network of foster homes. Besides providing a home environment for the dogs awaiting adoption, foster families help dogs recover from psychological and physical trauma, evaluate the dog's behavior, sometimes work on basic manners and obedience, and are a core component of the adoption process.

Finding Foster Volunteers

Existing volunteers are a great resource for recruiting new foster parents. Make literature available to your rescue's volunteers and encourage them to let neighbors, co-workers, club members, family, and friends know about your rescue's need for foster home volunteers. Current volunteers are your perfect spokespeople because they have a vested interest in the rescue. They also have a unique opportunity to talk with others about their experiences because they are seen around town with their foster dogs. Foster dogs are great conversation starters, especially if your foster dogs have vests or t-shirts that say "Adopt Me!" Encourage foster parents to keep a handful of business cards with them to hand out when they meet interested people.

Previous adopters also may be interested in becoming volunteers if they had a good experience with your rescue. Use your newsletter and Facebook page along with other social networking tools to stay in touch with previous adopters and let them know about foster home volunteer opportunities. New adoption applicants can be a resource for foster volunteers, too. Perhaps after they applied, they realized that they're not in a position for a permanent dog for whatever reason. Are they able to help you out short-term? If they don't feel they're emotionally ready to permanently adopt a dog, but you believe they would be good adopters, will you allow them to foster-to-adopt? This can be especially effective with your older and hard-to-place foster dogs.

In addition to leaning on people who are already involved with your rescue, you can recruit new foster parents by posting flyers at pet-related businesses, coffee shops, and on other community message boards. Target businesses that attract people who are dog-friendly and possibly interested in the breed you rescue, if you're a breed-specific rescue. For example, Weimaraners are active and bred as hunting dogs, so a Weimaraner rescue can target running stores, hiking clubs, and hunting and fishing businesses.

Please refer to *Chapter 10: Volunteers* for further ways to find and recruit foster volunteers.

Foster Qualifications

While you may look for certain unique characteristics in foster parents depending on whether you are a breed-specific rescue, there are some general traits to look for when evaluating foster parent applicants. One easy general question to ask is, "Would you leave your own dog alone with this person?" If the answer is no, you may want to suggest this person takes an alternate role with your rescue.

New foster volunteers need to go through the same reference and veterinary checks as people applying for adoption. You want to know if they are upstanding, responsible individuals who take appropriate care of their own pets and children before you give them one of yours. They should fill out a foster home application  similar to an adoption application. Potential fosters should be interviewed by someone who is well-versed in your standards of care. These standards should be discussed in a preliminary interview and reinforced in a foster welcome packet.

Rescues specializing in small breeds sometimes discourage fostering for people who have large-breed dogs at home. Because many large-breed dogs are docile and not necessarily dog aggressive, a better policy may be to have an experienced volunteer evaluate resident pets during the home check, noting if they have any preferences (e.g., may not be okay with other males, needs mellow dogs, etc.). A greater concern than size for many rescues is sex. (E.g., two female Boxers should not be put in the same home because they have a high propensity of fighting.) Whatever you decide on these topics, you should absolutely require that foster dogs are crated when left alone with resident pets. This is for both the safety of the foster pets and the safety of the resident pets.

Some rescues disqualify individuals from becoming foster parents because they don't have fenced yards. A blanket policy like this could eliminate some high-quality foster homes, so a better policy may be to evaluate applicants as individuals and make sure to place the right foster dogs with them. If a foster doesn't have a fenced yard but is committed to walking foster dogs several times a day, you should only place dogs with him or her that are willing to eliminate when on leash. If a foster has a lower fence than you normally require, have him or her sign a form stating that he or she will not let the dog in the yard unsupervised (this may be standard verbiage in your foster agreement) and do not give him or her dogs who jump. One yard item that should be non-negotiable is tethering. Dogs should not be tethered outside for any reason because the rope tethering the dog can be dangerous to him or her and because tethering is often a cause for dog fights. Additionally, some towns and cities have anti-tethering laws. If a foster has a history of tethering dogs, this needs to be addressed immediately. Tethering is a reasonable reason to reject an applicant.

Lastly, some rescues require that foster parents only foster for their rescue. Though not typically a deal breaker, the reasoning for this is sound. Consider the case where a family is fostering two different dogs from two different rescues. Both dogs suddenly become ill. Which rescue is responsible for the vet bills? If your potential foster parent has fostered for other rescues, you might ask which organizations he or she has worked with, and follow up with the organization to find out if he or she had any issues.

Your rescue should have a limit on the number of foster dogs or total dogs allowed in foster homes at one time. Key rescue personnel need to know and enforce these limits. This should be discussed up front with potential fosters, and those with too many dogs should be asked to volunteer in a capacity other than fostering.

If the applicant adequately responds to the questions on the application and passes the preliminary phone interview, the next step is to have a volunteer complete a home inspection. During the inspection, the experienced volunteer should evaluate both the home for any safety issues and the family – both human and animal members – to ensure everyone is comfortable with the idea of fostering and understands what is required of them. The process for evaluating a foster home should be similar to the process for evaluating an adopter, which is discussed in further detail in *Chapter 12: Adoption Process.*

First Steps for New Fosters

Once approved, a foster parent signs a foster agreement. This normally includes items such as a liability waiver in case of injury or damage to the humans, their own dogs, and their home; a statement that the foster dog remains the property of the rescue until it is adopted; and basic expectations regarding the care of the foster dog.

A comprehensive welcome kit in addition to the foster agreement will help foster families understand and remember what the rescue expects from them. This should include detailed information about expectations, common issues, and who to call for help. The following is a list of topics you may need to include in your welcome packet depending on the size of your rescue and its geographic sprawl:

- Information about your rescue
    - o Your mission
    - o Why your rescue exists
    - o What to expect the dogs to be like
    - o Volunteer opportunities
    - o Educational materials for volunteers to read and share

- Intake procedures
  - Bathing and grooming
    - Nail-trimming
    - Physical evaluation
      - Common physical abnormalities to look for
  - Evaluation process
    - How fosters should evaluate dogs
    - Who to contact about mild or serious issues
    - How long a foster should keep a dog for evaluation
  - Standard medical procedures
    - Vaccines, de-worming, and spaying/neutering
    - Microchips
    - Other standard medical procedures
    - Non-standard medical procedures
- Contact lists
  - Emergency contacts
  - Veterinary partners
  - Other foster families
  - Businesses that offer your volunteers discounts
- Tips on how to introduce new dogs to children and current furry family members
- Limits on allowable number of foster dogs (or total pets)
- Items provided to foster homes by the rescue
  - Leashes, collars, tags, bowls, food, crates, belly bands for housetraining issues, adoption kits, etc.

- Standards of care
  - How much/when/what to feed their foster dogs
  - Training expectations
    - Some rescues provide training assistance
  - Exercise
  - Veterinary emergency policy
  - Unadoptable dog procedure
    - What to do if a dog turns out to be terminally ill or has a severe behavior issue
  - Yard rules
    - Dogs should *never* be tethered or unsupervised
  - Lost dog procedures
- Pet data and listing for website, etc.
  - Dog evaluation form
  - Guidelines for writing a dog description
    - Name of dog, age, weight, background, likes and dislikes, current state (agitated, relaxed, etc.), ideal forever family traits
    - Description examples
    - Where they should send/post the description
  - Photo and video guidelines
- Adoption process
  - Adoption event policies
    - Foster parent expectations
    - Availability of transport and event volunteers to pick up and return dog from events

- o Application evaluation procedures
  - How to get applications
  - What to look for
- o Interview procedures
  - Questions to ask
  - Red flags
- o Home check procedures
- o Guidelines for accepting or turning down a potential adopter
- o Transport procedures
- Breaks
  - o Average length of time foster homes keep dogs and reasons for variations
  - o Transferring foster dogs to other foster homes
  - o How to request a break from fostering
- Foster "failure"
  - o Discounts given to foster homes for keeping foster dogs
  - o Adoption process for foster families to adopt foster dogs
- Permanent fosters
  - o Hospice care policies
  - o Reasons a dog would be unadoptable
- Financial expectations
  - o Policy on vet bills
  - o Policy on food/toys/treats/leashes/collars/tags/etc.
  - o Transportation costs
  - o Grooming costs

Some foster applicants will be dog *lovers* who don't have much dog experience, but lack of experience in itself should not be grounds for denying a person the opportunity to become a foster parent. A thorough welcome packet and helpful mentoring by an experienced foster parent can get any new foster parent up to speed quickly.

Information about your rescue: Do not take it for granted that your volunteers completely understand the reasons dogs come into your rescue. Knowing the reason your rescue exists will help your foster homes educate others about the importance of adoption and of carefully researching breed characteristics and care before getting a dog. This knowledge will also help them to evaluate potential adopters and to understand your decision-making process when difficult decisions must be made.

Bathing/grooming: Most rescues insist that fosters bathe every new dog who comes in, regardless of where they came from. The reason for this is that dogs can carry fleas, ticks, and other parasites. Bathing a dog not only reduces the chance that the foster family's own pets will be infected but also gives the foster parent an opportunity to look for any physical anomalies on the new dog.

Dog evaluation: Whether a foster parent is doing a formal or informal evaluation, a rescue should provide a foster family with guidelines of the "normal" temperament and behaviors for a rescued dog. Fosters need tips on how to work with common issues (leash aggression, food aggression, fear, jumping) and resources for dogs needing professional help, whether from a trainer or a veterinarian. They also need guidelines about what constitutes a "serious" issue.

Some rescues require fosters to keep dogs for a specified period of time before they are adopted. There are different schools of thought on this topic. The first says that it takes up to two weeks for most physical and behavioral issues to manifest themselves. Rescues following this philosophy may have several special, experienced foster homes that take in all new fosters for their first two weeks in the rescue in order to evaluate them. The second school of thought is that this rigid policy unnecessarily ties up foster homes. (E.g., when a family-surrendered dog with complete vet records comes into the rescue and is obviously ready for adoption.) The best policy is to look at dogs as individuals and treat them as such. Dogs of unknown origin may require a longer evaluation period than dogs with complete records. Instead of having a rigid time period that a foster must keep a dog, a rescue can consider adopting out a dog when the right fit comes along and then offering a two-week trial period for new adopters, which is discussed in greater detail in *Chapter 12: Adoption Process.*

Rescues should always require foster families to fill out a foster dog evaluation form, which they should periodically update as the dog grows and blossoms in their care. The rescue administration should keep this form on file after the dog is adopted in case the dog is returned or historical  information needs to be accessed for whatever reason. This form should include information about the dog's history, health, behavior, and microchip registration.

Exercise and dog parks: You will also want to include information in your welcome kit about exercise and dog parks. Some rescues recommend not taking foster dogs to dog parks at all, whereas others simply recommend that fosters thoroughly evaluate dogs for temperament and health issues before taking them to the dog park. While access to a yard is better than nothing regarding exercise, most rescues require that foster parents walk their foster dogs regularly on a leash. Walking is a fun way to exercise a dog, and it is an important part of the dogs' socialization process.

Feeding: You may recommend that foster homes feed dogs on a schedule instead of free-feeding to avoid overeating and food-fighting and to help foster dogs get on a schedule. This is especially important with dogs who need to be potty trained.

Financial expectations: All reputable rescues pick up the cost of veterinary care for foster dogs. Policies on who pays for food, supplies, transportation, and other items vary between rescues. Generally, if your rescue deals with many large-breed dogs, you might consider picking up the cost of food or providing food to your foster families. Most small-breed rescues don't bother because food is a fairly minimal expense for foster homes. Check with your accountant about whether foster parents can write off the purchases they make for their foster dogs.

Socialization

Some rescues do not have the opportunity to temperament test foster dogs before they go into a foster home, and even for those who can, it is impossible to predict exactly how a pet will behave in a new environment except to expect that he or she will most likely be a little disoriented and fearful. To minimize problems, have your experienced foster parents chime in on socialization tips for new foster dogs and include their advice in your welcome kit.

Many foster homes have resident dogs, cats, other pets, and children. This provides a great opportunity to socialize foster dogs without overwhelming them, but it can also cause challenges. Most organizations encourage foster parents to slowly introduce foster dogs to the other family members by keeping them crated or isolated for some period of time before being set free in the home. However, how a dog is introduced to a new home is dependent on who is living in that home, the dog's breed, and the dog's individual temperament.

Once foster dogs are introduced to their new foster family members, foster parents should keep notes on how the dog interacts. Is he or she fearful? Playful? Aggressive? Does he or she guard his or her food? Does he or she jump? Perhaps the foster dog is very easygoing and would do well in any environment. When ready, fosters might begin taking their foster dogs to local parks, dog parks (depending on your policy), meet-ups, pet supply stores, and other pet-friendly businesses where the foster dog will encounter other animals and humans. Some foster parents can take their foster dogs to work with them. It's important to remind foster parents to only take a foster dog to an off-leash area when they are completely confident that the animal is even-tempered.

Veterinary Care

One main piece of information that should not be overlooked is your expectations about veterinary care. Are you able to take care of medical items for foster dogs before you send them to foster homes, or will the foster parents be responsible for taking the dogs to the vet? Small rescues with foster homes located within a localized geographical region are usually able to take the dog directly to the veterinarian before placing him or her in foster care. This way, the veterinarian can check the dog over for any injuries, worms, growths, eye problems, and contagious diseases. Additionally, the rescue volunteer handling the initial veterinary visit can evaluate the dog for any obvious behavioral issues. This arrangement is beneficial because it facilitates fitting the right dog with the right foster home (e.g., not placing a cat-aggressive dog in a home with cats, a dog with sarcoptic mange in a home with other dogs, ect.). If most of your fosters use the same vet, you might want to have one volunteer who coordinates all vet visits so that your vets are not receiving calls from multiple people associated with your organization.

Rescues that cover a large geographic area often do not have the luxury of taking dogs for veterinary care before placing them in foster homes, so the responsibility usually rests with the foster family. These rescues should develop discount relationships with veterinarians in every area where they have foster homes and then require foster families to use those veterinarians for foster dogs. They often leave a credit card on file with the veterinarians, so the foster homes can provide their foster dogs with veterinary care as needed. In these cases, the foster parents must be able to evaluate their foster dog's health and personality themselves.

Many rescues order their medications and microchips in wholesale quantities and distribute them to foster families to keep on hand. Whether your foster parents are responsible for initial veterinary care or not, they should be made aware of your standard veterinary protocol, so they can inform adopters about the medical care the dog has received.

Training

The amounts of training foster parents are expected to provide varies from one organization to another. Some rescues expect their foster parents to work with dogs on basic obedience, while others are just happy for foster parents to provide food, water, shelter, and exercise. Obviously, rescues that have a large geographic sprawl can't expect foster parents to get together regularly for training. However, even for these types of organizations, training seminars can be conducted online at a reasonable cost.

For organizations that are geographically localized, regular training sessions help develop community in addition to training confidence and skills, let alone improving the adoptability of foster dogs. Ongoing training is important, no matter what level of experience a foster parent has. Even the most experienced foster parents run into new challenges, but through organized training sessions, these issues can be addressed in a timely manner and other fosters can learn from them, too.

Some local dog trainers are eager to help rescues. They are a good source of expertise in your training sessions. If you can't find a trainer to regularly work with your organization, consider inviting a variety of local trainers to conduct seminars for your rescue's fosters. Perhaps you can invite adopters and their newly-adopted dogs so that everyone can learn from each other. Invite your rescue's experienced volunteers to conduct training sessions if you can't get professional trainers to help. Some topics you might cover in addition to basic obedience include canine massage, cooking for dogs with allergies, food aggressions, barking at inappropriate times, potty training, Tellington Touch, etc. Decide on a timetable and location and then share that information with fosters, giving them enough time to plan to attend. Follow up on trainings with Facebook or message board discussions.

Whether you can provide regular training sessions for your volunteers or not, you may want to include some basic training tips in your foster welcome kit.

Foster Dog Listings

It's important to list your dogs online for potential adopters to see as soon as possible. Even if a dog is on a medical hold because of something like kennel cough, he or she should be listed immediately. Listing your not-yet-adoptable dogs may help you to raise funds for their care and develop interest in them for when they are healthy and ready for adoption.

Having the foster parent write the description of the dog works well because it takes something off someone else's plate, and it is the best way to get accurate data, especially if the foster parent regularly revises the information as the dog grows and blossoms in the foster home. Descriptions should include the dog's name, age, weight, background, likes and dislikes, current state (agitated, relaxed, etc), ideal forever family, etc. These descriptions should be honestly written and include photos and video of the dog. *Chapter 9: Marketing* lists suggested photo guidelines and more information about description-writing, which you may want to include in your foster welcome kit.

Adoption Events

Fostering is a lot of work in and of itself, so rescues should not expect foster families to take their adoptable dogs to events every weekend. Provide event and transport volunteers who can pick up and drop off foster dogs before and after events. *Chapter 12: Adoption Process* covers the adoption process in more detail, but it is important to note that dogs should not go home directly from adoption events with adopters who have not been thoroughly pre-screened.

Reviewing and Distributing Adoption Applications

It is the opinion of many experienced foster homes and established rescuers that foster parents should be heavily involved in the decision process for choosing an adoption applicant for their foster dogs because they know the dogs best. This means having an individual or committee screen incoming applications to ensure the applicant meets the rescue's general adoption criteria before distributing the qualified applications to foster homes with dogs who may fit the applicants' needs.

The process of application distribution is one of the most challenging parts of rescue management. How do you efficiently take in applications, review them, and distribute them to foster families of potential dogs that fit the needs of the applicants? How do you ensure applicants are being contacted by someone but not by too many people? How do you alert all fosters who have received an application when the applicant has adopted a dog from a different foster or when further information is uncovered that disqualifies a potential adopter from adopting? Who is ultimately responsible for following up and making sure all applicants have been contacted in a timely manner?

Many rescues use free Internet applications such as Google Docs or Dropbox to post their applications online for fosters to pull after some initial review process, which may be as thorough as giving the application a preliminary interview and home check or as preliminary as simply making sure all important fields are filled in and there are no glaring red flags. Other software to look into is Animal Shelter Manager and Sugar CRM. Whatever your rescue's process, it's important to explicitly explain to foster homes what your expectations are of them and to provide applications to foster parents in a timely manner.

Interviewing Potential Adopters

Some rescues ask a specific volunteer to conduct preliminary interviews to uncover more information about adopters who pass the initial application screening. Others have foster families complete an interview with adopters they see as a possible fit for their dogs. Either way, the purpose of an interview is to discover what a family is truly looking for, ensure everyone in the household is committed to caring for the dog, and uncover any issues that require further discussion or education. Foster parents are generally qualified to complete this sort of interview, especially because they can discuss their individual foster dogs with a family.

Some rescues make interviewing a two-step process, where one volunteer calls, interviews, and then writes a summary of the conversation to accompany the application when it is passed on to foster homes. This way, when the foster parent calls the applicant, the volunteer can focus the conversation on whether or not his or her foster dog is best suited for the applicant, and you can rest assured that someone has made initial contact with potential adopters, explained your process, and informed them that they will be contacted next when a potential good fit for their family is found.

Home Checks

Some rescues have specific volunteers initially evaluate each application and then pass the qualified applicants along to a home check volunteer. In this case, the applicant is completely qualified to adopt from your rescue before that the application moves along to the foster home application "pile." Other rescues leave the home check step until after a foster parent determines that a particular applicant might be a good fit for his or her foster dog. The applicant interview can be conducted before or during the home visit, but pre-screening applicants with an interview before scheduling a home visit is usually most efficient to ensure you are not wasting your time on uncommitted or unqualified applicants. The point of the home visit is to find out what a "day in the life" will be like for the dog being adopted out and to discover any issues before they become problems (e.g., family is not fully committed, there are problems with the fence, the family intends to leave the dog in the garage, etc.).

Similar to interviewing, home checks can be completed by "home check volunteers" or by foster parents. Because home checks require a significant time commitment (traveling to and from the visit and spending time with the adoption applicants at their homes), this can be a good task for volunteers who are retired and have a lot of time to give.

For rescues spread out geographically, the foster is often responsible for the home visit. If an applicant has already passed the phone interview and lives very far away, a rescue can call other rescues in the area and ask if one of their volunteers can complete the home check. A last resort is to do a virtual home visit, where the potential adopter sends video or photographs of where the pet will be living, their fenced yard (if they have one), different rooms in the house, etc. It is imperative that reference and vet checks are completed as part of any adoption process, but these checks become even more important when conducting a virtual home check in lieu of a live one.

Breaks from Fostering

Whenever a foster home asks for a reprieve, the rescue should grant it happily. Whether they have fostered one dog or 300 dogs, they have helped your rescue and deserve respect and gratitude. By respecting foster breaks, you have a much better chance that the foster will again open his or her doors to your needy dogs again after a time.

> **"Dog rescue is an absolute passion of mine, but fostering is the most rewarding part of rescue for me. I've been doing it for years different breeds, a few different rescue groups. I thrive on every moment of it. I've fostered well over 100 dogs now, and as many times as I've said, 'This is my last one,' I cannot seem to give it up." *-Shereen Raucci, Mile High Weimaraner Rescue***

The length of time a dog stays in foster care varies from region to region, rescue to rescue, and breed to breed. However, longstanding rescues can certainly give foster homes an idea of how long they can expect to have a dog. Additionally, rescues need some procedures in place for transferring a dog from one foster home to another, should a foster home require a break. Having a few committed short-term fosters is helpful for transitional periods when you are waiting for a foster home to become available.

Foster Adoption and Permanent Fosters

It's inevitable that foster families, at times, will decide they'd like to adopt their foster dogs. You'll often hear this jokingly deemed "foster failure." Some rescue organizations offer foster parents a discount for keeping foster dogs, while others feel that fosters should pay the same amount as adopters. Some organizations prohibit fosters from adopting their foster dogs, but this policy is counterproductive. If a foster family is a good fit for a foster dog and has the financial means to care for him or her, there is no reason not to let them keep the dog. You may lose them as a foster family, but you won't retain them for long anyway if you do not keep them happy.

Some dogs who come into rescue aren't adoptable for a variety of reasons, be it medical or behavioral. A foster home willing to provide hospice or sanctuary for a "permanent foster" should not be charged for that dog, and the rescue should be responsible for veterinary care for the life of the animal. In this case, the rescue normally retains custody of the dog.

Foster Financial Expectations

Most foster parents are not made of money, and they hold day jobs just like most people. In order to continue fostering with your organization, they usually need some sort of financial support. What you provide to foster homes is up to you, but the more you provide, the less barriers to fostering there will be. Rescues should at least cover veterinary bills, heartworm prevention, harnesses, leashes, crates, and grooming costs (for breeds that need their coats professionally trimmed). Most large-breed rescues also cover food and treats because that can be a significant expense.

Building Community

Whether your rescue is geographically centralized or spread out over a large area, try to provide as many opportunities for fosters to get together as you can. That may mean "virtual get-togethers" like a Yahoo list or a Facebook page just for foster parents, or that may mean monthly, quarterly, or annual events in every region your rescue services. However you do it, fosters should have the opportunity to get to know each and to learn from each other's experiences. By maintaining a "family" atmosphere among your volunteers (and adopters), you'll have a much higher volunteer retention rate, an easier time of fundraising, and a better support network when you need it.

Terminating Fosters

Sometimes things happen within the volunteer base that necessitates a volunteer or foster leaving the group. New fosters might find that fostering isn't for them, but they are afraid to say it. Other times a foster may be so emotionally affected by the work that he or she can no longer make good decisions about their foster dogs. If a foster home violates the tenants of the foster contract, a rescue leader must use discretion in deciding if the failure was on the foster's part or the organization's part. Some violations simply require re-training, while others are reason for termination.

When the decision is made to terminate a relationship with a foster parent, it should be done swiftly and politely. Simply ignoring the foster family is not the answer. That leaves people wondering what happened. The leadership of the rescue should contact the foster parents, delicately explain the situation, and let them go with the sentiment that the dissolution of the relationship is actually in everyone's best interest. Leave the door open, if possible, to review their situation in the future. Acknowledge their contributions to your organization. Most importantly, the person delivering the bad news should treat the foster as he or she would want to be treated in this situation. While dog rescue is, of course, about dogs, it is also about people. An angry ex-foster can be a liability to your organization, so terminations must be handled with the greatest of care.

Do:

- DO give foster parents all of the information they need to provide the best care for the dogs they are taking into their home.

- DO clearly define your expectations *in writing.*

- DO heavily involve the foster family in the adoption decision-making process.

- DO find ways to provide ongoing education and community involvement opportunities to your foster families.

- DO consider a dog's needs and a foster home's needs before placing a dog in foster care.

- DO use technology to simplify your application evaluation processes.

- DO provide foster families with instructions on how to best photograph their foster dogs and encourage them to write the dog's descriptions.

Don't:

- DON'T ignore problems that arise with foster families.

- DON'T turn down a foster home because of lack of experience with dogs.

- DON'T make unreasonable requests to foster homes like having them take their dogs to adoption events every weekend.

- DON'T expect fosters to spend their own money on the foster dogs they are housing.

Resources:

Rescuers Ring In: http://upforpups.org/2011/04/best-practices-foster-homes/

Language of Dogs DVD: http://www.amazon.com/Language-Dogs-Sarah-Kalnajs/dp/B000P28RXU

Management software

    Animal Shelter Manager software: http://sheltermanager.sourceforge.net/home.php

    Sugar CRM software: http://www.sugarcrm.com/crm/

Tellington Touch: http://ttouch.com

Chapter 12:
Adoption Process

There are many different ways for rescues to find adopters. Refer to *Chapter 9: Marketing* for an in-depth discussion of how to market your rescue to potential adopters, volunteers, and donors.

Your website is your most valuable tool to encourage people to adopt and to let potential adopters know what you expect of them. The best rescue websites prominently showcase adoptable dogs. The pages with adoptable dogs on them have a highly visible link to the rescue's adoption requirements and application. On these websites, the process is smooth and simple.

Many rescues say their best source of new adopters is former adopters, whether the same adopter is coming back for another pet, or that person has referred friends and family to you. By maintaining regular contact with former adopters, you can significantly increase your adoption rate.

Some large organizations run discounts and specials for adopting dogs, but smaller organizations generally avoid offering adoption discounts and specials, such as adopting two dogs for the price of one. These types of discounts tend to be viewed as a bad idea because they may cause people to take on more than they can handle. Some rescues, however, do charge less for older or harder-to-place dogs, and some offer a discount off the adoption fee for senior citizens (humans, not dogs), who want to adopt. While we all know that encouraging people to buy pets as gifts for others is a bad idea, some rescues allow people to purchase gift certificates as a more positive alternative. However, gift certificates should only be issued under the pretense that the recipient still has to pass your application, interview, and home check process. If he or she does not fit your requirements, the amount of the gift certificate will be kept as a donation or refunded (it's up to you, of course, how you want to handle it).

Adoption Applications and Preliminary Contact

No organization should allow a potential adopter to take home a pet before that adopter has filled out an application and received a home visit, live interview, and reference check. With that said, keep in mind that a well-planned, thorough adoption process should also be timely and achievable. People jokingly commenting that "adopting a dog from you was harder than adopting a child" are not necessarily paying your organization a compliment. If the process is too difficult or lengthy, it will turn people away, resulting in fewer dogs being saved and more being purchased at pet shops.

Few rescues charge non-refundable application fees, but it appears to be a topic many rescues are considering. A spam-blocker like a Captcha (the letter/ number combination most online forms require for submission these days) will significantly reduce spam, and making all your fields mandatory for submission  will eliminate many Looky-Lous who have no real interest in adopting. Whether you advertise your dogs on your website or through a listing service, the application link should be visible near the dog's photo and description, so people can easily apply online. At the very least, your application should be a form people can easily fill out online and should include the following:

- Contact info (name, phone, email, address, best time to call)

- Current household members and their ages (human, canine, and all other pets)

  o Are pets spayed/neutered?

  o What types of dogs do you have?

  o Does anyone in the household have allergies to dogs?

- References (veterinarian and friend/family)

- Own or rent

  o Renters: Especially if you are adopting out a large-breed dog, it is important you receive a signed document from the landlord stating that type and size of dog is allowed in the building. Some rescues require a copy of the lease to prove the renter is allowed to have the dog in question.

- Thoughtful questions

  o What will you do when you travel?

  o Where will the pet go if you are no longer able to care for him or her?

  o How long will the dog be left alone each day? Where will he or she be kept?

  o How much do you expect to spend annually on your pet?

  o If you don't have a fenced yard, how will you take the dog outside to eliminate?

  o How will you discipline the dog if he or she misbehaves (e.g., chews on something, pees in the house, etc.)?

  o Where will the dog sleep at night?

Dog preferences (male/female, age, activity level, size (for non-specific breed rescues)

Most rescues have an adoption coordinator who reviews the applications before they are distributed to foster homes. That coordinator should be aware of red flags that will cause an application to be denied, such as if the applicants have intact animals and refuse to spay/neuter them, if they want to keep the dog outside, if they rent and cannot provide documentation about pet approval from their landlord, or if someone in the home is not on board with adopting a dog. Having a fenced yard and/or fence height is a sticking point for many rescues, but on this topic you are doing a serious disservice to your dogs of you do not evaluate each situation individually. Not all dogs need a high fence, and not all people without a fence are unfit adopters. If the adopter is committed to walking the dog frequently and not allowing him or her to be unsupervised and tethered in a yard, fence height should not generally be a disqualifying factor. You should simply not allow him or her to adopt a dog who is a known fence jumper or who has difficulty eliminating while on leash.

Rescue volunteers should acknowledge receipt of applications within 24-48 hours. Some "dog people" find it difficult to relate to other humans, which is another reason to have an adoption coordinator or committee — a person (or persons) serving as the face and voice of the rescue to adopters. These people make initial contact with potential adopters, thanking them for applying, helping them fill in any missing information, and discussing any reasons why they may have been rejected for adoption in hopes they can be "brought up to your rescue's standards." Informing people of the reasons for rejection in circumstances where people are turned down to adopt from your rescue is just as important as approving people for adoption. Whether those people end up adopting from you or not, at least they haven't just been ignored, and often they simply need a push in the right direction to become good adopters. The adoption coordinator can steer a foster home toward a potential applicant, but the foster parent knows the dog best, so the foster parent should be trusted to make final decisions on which homes they choose for their dogs.

Interviews

Once an adopter has completed filling out the adoption application, it's time for a volunteer to call him or her for an interview. As previously stated, some rescues pass the potential adopter's application directly along to foster homes for the foster parent to conduct the interview, whereas others prefer to have a specific volunteer or committee conduct preliminary interviews. Either way, your volunteers need to know how to communicate with potential adopters. They need to calmly ask thoughtful questions to discover the adopter's needs and follow up with appropriate questions and comments if the adopter gives the "wrong answer."

"If you want quality volunteers, supporters, and adopters, you have to know how to connect with people. Even people you wouldn't adopt a dead snake to need to be handled kindly. Bad PR, even if it's coming from someone you declined to adopt to for very valid reasons, is still bad PR."
– *Sharon Sleighter, Legacy Boxer Rescue*

If a foster parent or the designated interviewer is unsure about whether an applicant will be a good adopter after interviewing him or her, they should know what procedure to follow to escalate concerns. The procedure can be as simple as calling on another foster parent for a second opinion, voicing concerns to a committee, or posing questions to an internal online message board. Diverse opinions are helpful, but if the adoption is still questionable, it may be worth moving on to the next step before absolutely denying a dog to a potential adopter – the home check.

Home Checks

The next step after a phone interview is a home check, just like you would do for new potential foster homes, as was discussed in *Chapter 11: Foster Home Mangement.* Home checks are conducted in many different ways. For rescues that are spread out, they are sometimes done virtually. Some rescues have the foster parents complete home checks, in which case they often bring along their foster dogs to see how the dogs react. Other rescues send a specific home check volunteer with his or her own dog or no dog at all. Bring a dog is always a good idea because the volunteer can gauge the family member's reactions to him or her, as sometimes actions speak louder than words.

Home visits should include a careful inspection of the home and yard to ensure there is nothing that will put a dog in danger (e.g., breaks in the fence, wide fence slats, open steps, etc.). A volunteer should look for the following items and then fill out a home check report:

- Fence (walk entire fence line)
    - Made of solid material
        - Chain link is often unacceptable because many dogs can easily climb it.
        - Electric fences are completely unacceptable because predators can get in, but dogs can't get out.
    - Secure with no loose boards
    - Touching the ground and not patched with rocks and cinderblocks
    - At least five-feet high
        - Some rescues require six-feet.
    - Free of any furniture or features that dogs could easily use to jump it
    - Free of holes or gaps
    - Locking mechanisms on gates
        - Usually suggested but not mandatory

- Yard
    - Reasonably groomed
    - Free of obvious choking and poison hazards (including poisonous plants)
        - No children's toys, junk, accessible trash bags, and cigarette butts
    - No exposed plastic or metal edging that could cut a dog
    - Area for dog to eliminate

- House
  - o Reasonably clean
  - o Free of obvious choking and poison hazards (including poisonous plants)
    - ▪ No swallow-able children's toys, junk, office supplies, cigarette butts, etc.
  - o No exposed wires
  - o Garbage cans are inaccessible to dogs
  - o Dog crate is out of direct sunlight
  - o Dog has easily accessible water source
    - ▪ A toilet is *not* an acceptable water source!
  - o Basement access is limited or basement is free of hazards
  - o Cleaning supplies, detergent, and medicines are kept in inaccessible places
  - o Family has a screen door or a plan to prevent dog from dashing outside when someone comes in

The following items should also be discussed:

- Appropriate food and treats for dog
- Foods poisonous to dogs, including chocolate, onions, grapes, and raisins (get a complete list from ASPCA Animal Poison Control Center)
- Plants poisonous to dogs (see above)
- Appropriate places to leave the dog when no one is home (not left in a garage or yard or tied up anywhere)

When the home visit is complete, the volunteer needs to decide if the family is suitable for one of your rescue's dogs. A good question for the volunteer to ask him or herself is: "Would I leave my dog in this home?" Whatever the answer, a volunteer should contact the family within 24-48 hours to follow up and let the family know whether or not their home passed the home check. If the family fails the home check, they should be given the opportunity to bring their home "up to standards" whenever possible, or at least they should be politely informed of the reasons why their home didn't pass the inspection.

Declining Adopters

If the family fails the application process, interview, or home check, they should be given the opportunity to bring themselves "up to standards" whenever possible, or at least they should be politely informed of the reasons why they are not able to adopt from you. The best way to frame these kinds of conversations is, "The rescue believes it is in your best interest not to adopt a dog from us because..." Do your best not to place blame and not to alienate the applicant.

Some rescues keep a "Do Not Adopt" (DNA) list of people they believe are dangerous to animals. These names can be gathered from adoption applications, other organizations, criminal records, and newspaper articles. There are any number of reasons a rescue may decide to add a person to this list, which may include people who are known to have psychological disabilities resulting in hording, people who would kill their pets rather than contact a rescue or shelter for help, and people with a history of domestic violence.

Introductions

Some dogs have no problem allowing new dogs into their territory. However, if there is any question of a possible personality conflict, a good way to introduce dogs to their potential new canine family members is outdoors in a neutral area to avoid altercations due to territoriality. Walking the dogs on leash together can be a good introduction, and if neither dog is known to be aggressive, moving them into an off-leash fenced-in area is helpful. Depending on the breed, some rescues don't allow two females to live together in the same home, with some occasional exceptions.

Adoption Fees

It's unrealistic to think that adoption fees will cover the costs of preparing a rescued dog for adoption. Of course, some dogs (like the occasional healthy family surrender) come into rescue already altered and up-to-date on shots, but most dogs need to be altered and vetted, at the very least. Some need extensive surgeries, and as a rescue, it's your duty to do whatever you can for them within accordance to the policies your organization has set forth.

The purpose of the adoption fee is to supplement some of the costs of rescuing and to ensure the adopter is serious about getting a dog and understands the financial obligations associated with caring for a dog. Most rescues charge more for puppies and less for older dogs. Some have a flat fee, while others adjust their fees according to the age and/or health of the dog. Rescues most commonly charge between $100 and $400.

Adoption fees are considered program service revenue, which is exempt from federal income tax. Whether or not an adoption fee is subject to state sales tax is determined on a state-by-state basis. Some states assess sales tax on adoption fees of animals adopted out through non-profit rescue groups, while other states do not. For example, Minnesota adoption fees are subject to sales tax, while in Texas, adoption fees are considered exempt transactions. Rescues should review the laws of the states in which they operate. Each state's department of revenue has a comprehensive website listing good, reliable, accurate tax information for non-profits. Regardless of the state in which your rescue is based, you must keep clear and accurate financial records in case of an audit.

Adoption Contracts

Once you have approved a family to adopt and they have decided on a dog, they should fill out an adoption contract. An adoption contract should be designed to protect the dog, your organization, and the adopter. It should include clear expectations for care and treatment of adopted dogs and information

on the consequences of not upholding the standards outlined in the contract. You can further protect your dogs by including a clause stating that the rescue reserves the right to visit and check up on the dog at any point and to reclaim the dog if the rescue determines the dog is not being cared for according to the contract's standards. Contracts should be written using standard legal terms.

Consider the two following statements:

- Adopter promises to love the dog.

- Adopter agrees to yearly veterinary check-ups and to providing adequate nutrition, water, shelter, and exercise as directed by a board-certified veterinarian.

The second statement is *measurable,* whereas the first is not. Contractual requirements should be measurable.

Common adoption contract requirements cover the following topics:

- Veterinary visits and medical care

  o Vaccines

  o Heartworm preventative

- Food, water, shelter, supervision, exercise

- Abide by local dog laws

  o Licensing

  o Identification

  o Leash laws

- Communications with rescue

  o Update contact info upon moving

  o Notify rescue if dog is lost, stolen, or incapacitated

  o Contact rescue for assistance or counseling with behavioral issues

- o Return dog to rescue if adopter can no longer care for dog for any reason
- Indoor/outdoor policies
  - o Depends on breed and individual dog; many should not be left unsupervised in a yard for long periods of time
  - o Fence requirements, if any
- No tethering
  - o Nowhere; not in a yard or outside a store
- Hold harmless clauses
  - o Protects rescue from liability once dog is adopted
- Inspection
  - o Rescue may follow up on a dog at any point in time
- Trial period and return policy (see below)
  - o Duration of trial period
  - o Refunds and/or fees associated with returns
- Consequences
  - o What happens if terms are not upheld

A rescue should also keep documentation on information shared with potential adopters about any pre-existing health conditions and/or behavioral issues a dog may have. Additionally, it is a good idea to ask all adopters to outline what they will do if they become unable to care for their new pet. If the adopter has a clear plan for a friend or family member to care for the animal, this may preempt the need for the adopter to return his or her pet to the rescue upon becoming incapacitated.

Trial Period

Most rescues give adopters a two-week trial period to get to know their new dogs. The official trial period begins after the adoption contract is signed by the adopter and the rescue has collected the money for the dog. Some rescues will not cash the check for the adoption fee until the trial period is over, and they are sure the dog is a match with the family. Adopters should be advised that during this period, there is no shame in returning a dog if he or she is not a good fit. The rescue should make every effort to find adopters who return a dog a different dog, unless there is a good reason the organization decides it no longer wants to adopt to this person.

Most rescues offer a full or partial refund if the dog is returned during the trial period. A full refund is usually the best policy because you don't want any barriers to stand in the way of a dog who is not a good fit being returned. If a dog is returned after the trial period ends, there is usually no refund.

Adoption Kit

Giving the new dog adopters an adoption kit ensures that they have all of the information they need to care for their new dog. An adoption kit also protects the rescue, since the rescue can prove that it provided important information, such as veterinary paperwork, to the adopters. Your adoption kit may include all or part of the following:

- Breed information
- Adoption contract
- Dog profile (foster parent form – see *Chapter 11: Foster Home Management*)
- Veterinary paperwork
- Coupons
- Pet insurance information (in case they want to buy insurance for their new pet)
- "Personal Items" (collar, harness, leash, toys, etc.)
- Recommended food (sample, coupon, or information)

Do:

- DO advertise your rescue's adoptable dogs in a variety of ways.
- DO have a separate adoption application and contract.
- DO train volunteers how to conduct home visits.
- DO provide a list of food and plants that are poisonous to dogs to your home check volunteer, as well as a list of other dangerous things to look for.
- DO develop a safe method for your foster dog and pets at the potential adopter's home to meet before the adoption is finalized.
- DO have a trial period.
- DO create an adoption kit to give adopters.

Don't:

- DON'T leave anything about the adoption process up to chance.
- DON'T be afraid to turn down a potential adopter if you don't think the adopter and the dog aren't a good fit.
- DON'T turn down a family just because they have never had a dog before.
- DON'T be judgemental if an adopting family returns a dog to your rescue.

Resources:

ASPCA Animal Poison Control Center:
http://www.aspca.org/pet-care/poison-control/

Chapter 13:
Transporting Animals

Many rescue groups cover broad geographic areas and require transport volunteers to move dogs between surrender sites (puppy mills, shelters, relinquishing homes, etc.), foster homes, rescue events, and adopters. Many require people who are surrendering their dogs to deliver them in person or at least to pay for transport, and some require adopters to pick their new pets up in person. Other rescues feel that if an adopter passes a home visit, interview, and reference checks, the adopter doesn't need to go to the foster home in person. If this is the case, the rescue will collaborate with the adopter to transport the dog to its new home.

Safe transport means more than just having a driver and a vehicle. Transportation volunteers must be aware of a dog's needs. They need emergency contact numbers and should provide the following during the transport:

- Heat or air-conditioning depending on outside temperature

- Safety (seat belt, crate, etc.)

- Food and water (depending on the distance of the trip)

- Potty breaks

- Separation mechanism if transporting multiple animals

- Medication doses (if necessary)

- Veterinary records

- Surrender papers

- Adoption kit items (when necessary)

For local or in-state rescue, many groups rely on local volunteers. Some groups even have an appointed transport coordinator and a specific group of volunteers who are on call to help with transports. Most are asked to use their own vehicles and in most cases are not reimbursed for gas or other expenses. (Some state laws allow 501(c)3 non-profits to offer a tax deduction for vehicle expenses when transporting rescue animals.)

Long-distance transport is a world of its own and without these transporters, the number of dogs saved would be far less than it is today. Long-distance transports are made using private vehicles, rental vans, or even airplanes! Rescues also rely on over-the-road truckers who often let a rescued dog or two ride along. When it comes to getting a dog safely to your rescue, you will find that sometimes creativity is key. The best place to start, however, is to reach out to your own volunteers and established transport organizations first, some of which we have listed in the resources section of this chapter. Note that these organizations generally rely on donations, just like you, and that you shouldn't expect them to transport your dogs for free. Find out what their recommended donation is per transport. It is usually very reasonable, as they exist to help you save lives.

If you are using your own volunteers for transport, they should fill out the same volunteer application as any other volunteer, although you may take the additional step of obtaining driving record information. Public records searches can be performed easily online. All transport volunteers should receive a document highlighting the aforementioned transportation topics, as a dog's safety should always be your first and foremost concern. Check with a lawyer about your liability if a volunteer gets in a car crash and/or an animal is injured.

Do:

- DO be open-minded and creative about ways to get a dog from his or her former home, shelter, or puppy mill to a foster- or forever-home.

- DO consider the dog's safety and welfare above anything else.

- DO check to make sure the transport vehicle has heat or air conditioning, depending on the outside temperature, and is safe.

- DO periodically check your transport volunteer's driving records.

- DO consider partnering with established transport organizations.

Don't:

- DON'T allow a dog to be transported in a vehicle without taking the proper safety measures.

- DON'T neglect to provide information to transport volunteers about your transportation standards.

- DON'T miss out on a great adopter because of geographic concerns; transport volunteers and organizations are available to help you.

Resources:

Rescuers Ring In: http://upforpups.org/2011/05/best-practices-transporting-animals/

List of transport organizations: http://themuddypuddle.com

Transportation message boards:

Dog Rescue Railroad: http://dogrescuerailroad.org/

Meetup.org: http://eCa.sh/JDUw

Transport organizations:

All Paws Transport (From the South to the Northeast): http://allpawstransport.com/

C.A.R.E. Transport (KS, MO, OK, AR, NM, NE, CO): www.caretransport.org

Pilots n' Paws (National): http://pilotsnpaws.org

Rescue Riders (AL, TN, KY, OH, PA, NY, CT, VT and NH): http://www.rescueriderstransport.com/

Chapter 14:
Humane Education

While the main mission of a dog rescue is to help dogs find their forever homes, regardless of where they lived before, there is a second mission to consider – that of promoting the right of *every* dog (and animal) to be treated humanely.

Because rescues are constantly in the public's eye, they have a great opportunity to reach out even to those who are not in the market for a new dog with information about the humane treatment of animals. Rescue volunteers can do more than lead by example; they can inspire others by educating them about what drives them for the important animal welfare work they do.

In a nutshell, a *humane* person is one who shows great compassion, tenderness, and caring for others, including animals, and who tries whenever possible to alleviate another's suffering. Not only does this message positively affect the victims of animal neglect and abuse, but it also has a positive impact on those who take the leap to stand up for our furry friends. If you are reading this book, you understand what this means: Doing the right thing for animals can be difficult at times, but the rewards far outweigh the burden.

Rescues can promote the humane treatment of animals in several ways:

- Leading by example
  - o Encourage adopters to train their dogs to be therapy dogs and then to take them out in the community and show off their skills.
  - o Show your support of other organizations that promote the humane treatment of animals.
  - o Treat your own animals humanely.

- Events and outings

  o Make sure your volunteers understand what you rescue stands for and are armed with interesting animal welfare topics to discuss at events.

  o Have pamphlets on different animal cruelty topics available to hand out.

  o Be ready to discuss your dogs' stories at events, out on the trail, in stores, wherever your dog can draw some attention to him- or herself. (E.g., when people question why your puppy mill survivor is cowering and looking petrified, take the opportunity to explain the relationship between pet shops and puppy mills.)

  o Sponsor a program to introduce some of your rescued dogs to schools, libraries, daycares, youth groups, scout groups, adults in assisted living centers, etc.

- Media

  o Reach out to newspapers, magazines, radio stations, and online sources to publicize your adoptable pets.

  o Establish yourself as an expert in animal welfare and offer to discuss welfare-related topics. This may mean writing a newspaper article or blog post or being interviewed on a radio show.

- Online

  o Share information about the proper care of dogs and other advocacy issues via Twitter, Facebook, and other social media networking tools.

  o Prominently link from your rescue's website to other sites that educate about topics like puppy mills, breed-specific legislation, dog fighting, and other animal welfare topics. There are many great websites out there, some of which are referenced in the Resources section of this chapter.

o Comment on blogs that discuss animal welfare issues, especially those written by people who are obviously misled.

Humane Education Topics

There are several different topics that fall under Humane Education. Fortunately, rescues don't have to be experts on each of these topics because so much information is available. Research the topics that are most closely related to your rescue's mission, and be sure to incorporate information about those topics into all of your outreach programs:

- Breed characteristics

  o Especially if you are a purebred rescue, informing people about your breeds attributes and quirks can help the breed overall. (E.g., Border Collies are notorious for nipping people's heels, but that behavior is simply a result of their breeding. People should only adopt Border Collies if they understand the dog's herding needs.)

  o Educate people about how to choose the right breed, age, temperament, etc. for themselves and their families.

- Breed-specific legislation

  o Explain the fallacy of thinking that banning breeds makes communities safer, and instead encourage people to learn how to recognize the signs of animal abuse.

- Human irresponsibility

  o In what ways are humans blaming dogs, when the dogs' behavior is truly a reflection of how they are being raised? How can humans change their behavior to better socialize and train their dogs?

  o Educate people about realistic expectations in animal guardianship, such as time commitment, financial obligations, proper feeding, veterinary care, exercise, and other facets of proper canine care.

o Encourage the benefits of professional training; many times it's the person, not the dog, who needs training!

o Teach people how to understand dogs and to appreciate how dogs positively impact their everyday life.

o Teach people how to identify signs of animal abuse and how to get help.

- Local legislation regarding animal issues

o Get to know your local animal welfare initiatives and which decision-makers are your champions. Let people know about them, as well as the decision-makers who may be misled. Encourage people to contact them and help them see the importance of protecting animals.

o Support local ballot initiatives regarding animal welfare by helping to collect signatures.

- Spay/neuter

o Discuss the benefits of spaying and neutering dogs and dispel misconceptions.

o Provide a list of low-cost clinics.

- Pet first aid

o Prepare first aid kids and sell them or hand them out at events. These can contain information pieces on such topics as what to do if you dog is bit by a rattlesnake, has a seizure, eats poisonous foods or plants, etc.

- Puppy Mills and pet shops

o Support awareness about puppy mills and backyard breeders. Talk about where the cute puppies in pet stores usually come from (puppy mills).

Even though you are involved with dog rescue, it's worth noting that your humane education program should encourage kindness to all animals, not just dogs. While the topic of speciesism is very controversial, the fact is that farm animals die for us to live, and no matter what you believe about their intellects, this fact should be respected. Supporting businesses that slaughter their animals as humanely as possible (e.g., certified cruelty-free), encouraging people to buy non-leather alternatives when possible (e.g., canvas shoes instead of leather shoes), and simply reminding others of the sacrifices these animals make for us is a step in the right direction.

> "Even if groups don't take on speciesism actively, simply having a policy that the rescue will not pay for or encourage any form of animal abuse (not just against dogs and cats) is a good start. This means not having fundraisers where the group is making money from promoting animal abuse (selling meat/dairy/eggs, animal skins, hunting/fishing packages, gifts baskets with products tested on animals in them, etc.) and encouraging people to consider the impact human choices have on *all* animals, not just dogs and cats." –*Dallas Rising, Small Dog Rescue of MN*

Educating the Next Generation

Helping children develop empathy for animals benefits them in both their relationships with animals and with humans. Therefore, part of an animal welfare organization's focus should be on bringing messages about the humane treatment of animals to children. Rescue organizations don't have to reinvent the wheel to reach out to youngsters. The Humane Society of the United States and its local humane societies provide a free classroom program for children. Educating children can be as simple as getting them involved in fundraising events, helping foster parents to involve their children in the adoption process, and taking kid-friendly rescued dogs to schools and events where there are many children and using the dog as a discussion piece about animal welfare topics. For some of this outreach work you may need a rescue dog who has obtained his or her therapy dog status, but that shouldn't be hard to do. Many rescued dogs excel at therapy dog training.

Benefits of Humane Education

Some rescuers become overwhelmed with the day-to-day tasks of taking in dogs and adopting them out, and they lose sight of the importance of reaching out beyond the people who have contact the rescue to get a new dog. However, the thing to keep remembering is this: Wouldn't you like to live in a world where rescues and shelters were only needed to re-home dogs who are surrendered by people because of dire circumstances? Wouldn't it be nice to see the day when you can sleep soundly at night knowing that there are not hundreds of thousands of dogs languishing in cages – completely legal cages – simply for the sake of human greed and ignorance? If, as rescuers, we reach beyond just moving dogs along the conveyor belt and truly change people's hearts and minds, this day *can* come.

Here are some other reasons why reaching out to others, teaching them about the importance of caring for animals, and showing them what they can get in return, is so important.

- Build moral character.
    - o Understanding the needs of animals and interacting with them helps people develop compassion, empathy, ethics, and most importantly, it reinforces the Golden Rule: Do unto others as you would have them do unto you.

- Create responsible and caring citizens.
    - o Humane education helps people examine and understand the consequences of their behaviors and choices through discussions of proper and improper treatment of pets.

- Reduce violence.
    - o People who display violence to animals often go on to engage in violent acts toward their peers and sometimes even carry these behaviors into adulthood.

- Cultivate empathy for animals.

  o Humane education helps people understand that animals are living, feeling beings who deserve to be treated with respect and compassion.

- Empower people to make a difference.

  o Engaging in animal welfare activities or simply understanding the topics surrounding animal welfare helps people develop a sense of control within their environments and learn ways in which they can help solve problems rather than create them.

If you, who so passionately believes in animal welfare that you put aside your own life to advocate for animal welfare, don't reach out to teach others to care for animals, to teach them empathy and responsibility for our "best friends," who will? If your words and actions can make a difference in how people treat their animals, then you are creating positive change that will ripple throughout your community and reach far beyond, and *that* is what will ultimately decrease the number of dogs who need saving. In the meantime, keep up the great work, save as many dogs as you can, and don't forget to give people a nudge to get involved or at least to treat their best friends better, when you see the opportunity.

Do:

- DO use existing materials or create your own to educate others about animal welfare.

- DO encourage your volunteers and adopters to set a good example for others.

- DO take the message to children in classrooms, scouting meetings, libraries, etc.

- DO use creative avenues like radio talk shows and blogs to discuss the humane treatment of animals.

Don't:

- DON'T think that your rescue's mission ends with the re-homing of dogs. There is much more "good" you can accomplish through humane education initiatives in addition to your adoption activities.

- DON'T assume children are too young to learn about humane treatment of animals.

- DON'T assume that people understand the topics that are so close to your heart. Tell them about animal welfare!

Resources

Best Friends outreach: http://www.bestfriends.org/atthesanctuary/humaneeducation/classroomresources.cfm

For Pit's Sake: http://www.forpitssake.org/

Hand N' Paw learning website: http://www.artforpaws.net/humaneeducation.html

Happy Tails Books: http://happytailsbooks.com

HSUS child outreach program: http://www.humanesociety.org/parents_educators/

Mill Dog Manifesto: http://upforpups.org/mill-dog-manifesto-ebook/

National Humane Education Society: http://www.nhes.org/

PetStation Guide to Natural & Enlightened Petkeeping http://www.petstation.com/

Unchain Your Dog: http://www.unchainyourdog.org/Teachers.htm

Chapter 15:
Special Situations

Information provided to rescues by surrenderers when giving up a dog is usually subjective at best. The surrenderer may say that the dog is wonderful, kind, housetrained, good with children, polite to other animals, and healthy. But even if those things are true, newly-displaced dogs tend to act differently than they did in their previous environments, at least during a transition period that could last a few days or a few months.

Unfortunately, many dogs who end up in rescue have special needs. Dogs from puppy mills and abuse/neglect situations tend to be fearful and skittish, in addition to having a host of medical issues. Some are friendly and just happy to be out of their previous situations, but more often than not, dogs from these situations need some special TLC.

This chapter offers an overview of some special situations your organization is likely to encounter. For a more in-depth discussion of the following situations, check out the links in the Resources section.

Puppy Mill Survivors

Puppy mill dogs come into rescue with various medical, physical, and emotional challenges. Some mill dogs have major medical issues that must be taken care of immediately. At the least, almost all incoming mill dogs need to be spayed/neutered and brought up to date on shots. Mill dogs have emotional issues in varying degrees from spending years locked in small cages at the mill.

If your rescue takes in mill dogs, you should provide your foster families with information about how to support mill dogs through their difficult transition from cage to home, and inform them about typical issues they may encounter. One can never speculate about how long a foster home will need to keep a mill dog because each one is an individual and has different needs. Often foster homes need to get creative with their mill dogs to help them over fears such as going through doorways and down stairs. Much of the rehabilitation process is trial and error; the foster families must be persistent, observant, and flexible in order to discover the best ways to reach out to their mill dogs.

Mill dogs are almost always a flight risk. They will be scared in their new homes and should therefore be monitored at all times. Fosters should use a leash even when taking the dog outside into a fenced yard and should only take dogs for walks through a door leading into a fenced yard for an extra degree of protection against flight risk. Many rescues recommend harnesses for mill dogs because they can't back out of them like they can with collars.

Leash-walking: Leash-walking is a new experience for mill dogs and can be very frightening. Often they either try to bolt or flatten to the ground, refusing to walk. Getting a dog used to a harness and leash can be a long, frustrating process. A good way to teach a dog about leashes is to hook the leash onto his or her harness and then let him or her drag it around the house. This helps the dog get used to the weight and noise of the leash. Then, after a time, someone can hold gently onto the leash while it's attached to the dog and let the dog lead that person around the house. Go wherever the mill dog goes, and then gradually work up to using the leash to control where the dog goes. This can take a long time for some puppy mill dogs. After the dog is comfortable with guidance on a leash inside the house, your foster can try walking the dog in the yard. Fosters should never use a flexi-leash with a dog who may be a flight risk. If the foster were to drop the flexi, it would make a loud noise, scaring the dog and causing him or her to bolt.

Feeding: Mill dogs are often underweight and afraid to eat. Sometimes they have to be hand-fed, whereas other times they won't touch their food unless you pour it on the floor and/or leave the room.

Here are some tips for feeding mill dogs:

- If the mill dog won't eat out of a bowl, try a plate. If that doesn't work, scatter the food on the floor.

- If the dog won't eat in your presence, turn your back. If that doesn't work, leave the room. Gradually work up to where the dog lets you be in the same room while he or she eats. Mix dry dog food with canned or fresh cooked chicken, tuna, pumpkin, liverwurst, or hamburger.

- Mill dogs may be food-aggressive. Feed the dog separately from the other dogs in the house until you see how it reacts. You can put the mill dog's food in his or her crate or in a separate room.

Socialization: Mill dogs most likely don't know what it is like to be touched kindly by a human. They don't know how to behave inside a house and won't understand basic commands. In many cases, the foster home's family dogs can help mill survivors understand that the new humans in their lives are there to help, and they can also help teach the dogs how to behave in the house. The mill dog, having never lived in a house, won't know how to go up and down stairs, how to walk on wood floors, how to go through doorways, and how to respond to many other normal household activities and sounds. The foster home's family dogs show the mill dog – and any other foster dog – how to maneuver around the house and how to react to different sounds, people, and experiences. Dogs learn so much from each other, and it's no different for a puppy mill dog. The mill dog will watch how the foster family interacts with their own dog and how the family dogs behave in the house and at feeding time.

Puppy mill survivors have different ways of coping with their new world. Some become hyperactive and excited that they are out of the horrible puppy mill, while others may retreat to a quiet space in the house to block out the activity around them, seeming as though they wish to disappear. All dogs should have a safe place to go when they get overwhelmed, but use caution with mill dogs. You don't want them to spend all their time in a cage. They need to learn how to live in a home with people who love them. Don't rush them. Let them become comfortable in their new surroundings in their own time. Take things slowly and don't except changes overnight, but at the same time, help the dog to take small steps toward becoming more confident.

As mill dogs become more trusting of their foster parents, the parents should begin exposing them to new experiences. Mill dogs benefit by slowly being exposed to offices, stores, coffee shops, parks, friends' houses, etc., and while the dog will most likely show signs of fear at first, the ultimate outcome will be growth. If the dogs aren't aggressive towards adults and children, it's good to instruct people to sit near mill dogs and scratch under their chins. If the dog is treat-motivated (many are not, as they have never seen a treat), new people can offer them treats while petting them.

Taking puppy mill dogs out in public once they begin to trust you is good for both the dog and the community, as people need to understand what goes on behind the scenes of the puppy trade. Allowing people to meet your puppy mill survivors and hear their stories is a great way to educate others about the horrors of puppy mills and why people shouldn't buy from pet stores, which almost always get their puppy stock from puppy mills.

Fostering puppy mill survivors may sound like a lot of work, but many foster families feel that rehabilitating mill dogs is extremely rewarding. As the dogs improve, foster parents get to experience constant small victories, which are easily overlooked or seen as annoying in "normal" dogs. Examples of these small victories include the first time a puppy mill dog gets into the car by him- or herself, the first time he or she jumps up on the couch, and the first time he or she comes back inside from the yard without needing encouragement. These are all huge accomplishments for most mill dogs, and they are a lot of fun to celebrate.

Deaf and Blind Dogs

Being deaf or blind doesn't hinder a dog's ability to be a wonderful pet. Fosters and adopting parents need a little more patience and attention to detail with deaf and blind dogs, but other than that, they are just like any other dogs. Regardless of what a surrenderer says, a veterinarian should evaluate the extent of the dog's blindness and/ or deafness before the dog is placed up for adoption, so you can fully disclose the dog's condition to potential adopters. The dog may be able to hear certain wavelengths, such as whistles, but not a human's voice. The dog may have partial sight, like being able to see shadows, or he or she may be completely blind. An accurate assessment of the dog's challenge helps foster parents choose the best ways to communicate with blind and with deaf dogs.

Most deaf dogs can learn commands via hand signals. However, because of their disability, fosters need to keep them leashed at all times when not fenced-in and shouldn't leave them unattended at any time, even if the dog is just scouting the backyard. On the other hand, blind dogs may be able to walk on off-leash trails if they are reliably responsive to voice commands, but they still require intense supervision.

Both deaf and blind dogs may startle easily if another dog sniffs their behinds unexpectedly. Advising foster homes of this fact can help avoid unnecessary snapping or fighting. With the proper care, both deaf and blind dogs can be great family pets and can ease into new environments with minimal extra concern. During the first few visits to a new home, blind dogs should be walked around it on leash, so they can get their bearings. Once the dogs learn where things are – and these things aren't moved to other locations – they usually become so adept at navigating the home that it seems as though they can actually "see" where they are going. If items are moved in the house – at Christmas time, for example, when the sofa is moved to make room for a Christmas tree – it's best to go back to the leash training, so the dogs can quickly regain their bearings.

Amputees

Dogs with severe injuries or physical abnormalities requiring amputation occasionally come into rescue. Sometimes these abnormalities are birth defects, and other times they result from infection, illness (e.g., mast cell tumors), or physical trauma. Whatever the reason, at times, a veterinarian will recommend the removal of a dog's body part. While it is normal to feel emotional about approving the removal of a dog's body part, you should not hesitate to approve this if it will help the dog to live a longer and less painful life. Dogs tend to adapt quickly to life as amputees, much more quickly than many humans.

With severely injured dogs, you need to consider each case and decide on what is a reasonable amount of money to spend to save the life of the dog. What is the prognosis? Is amputation an option? Will the dog live long enough to enrich an adopter's life for a reasonable amount of time? What are the alternatives? These are always difficult decisions, but consulting with your vet and your Board of Directors can help. If you keep in mind that your ultimate goal is to do the most good for individual dogs and your rescue as a whole, you will make the right decisions.

Severe Behavior Issues

Many people think of biting as the only severe behavior issue. However, adopting out dogs with separation anxiety, chewing tendencies, obsessive-compulsive disorder (it happens in dogs, too), and other "quirks" can be very challenging. Unless a dog's undesirable behaviors pose a true risk to society (e.g., unpredictable aggression toward humans), a rescue should make every effort to move him or her toward an adoptable state before deciding on making the dog a permanent foster or euthanizing him or her. Behavior modification is often expensive in time, but if you can find a kind-hearted trainer who will extend a discount to your rescue (or better yet, foster your special-needs dogs), changing a dog's behavior does not necessarily need to be financially intensive.

Adopting Out Special Needs Dogs

Some rescued dogs have medical or emotional issues that are easily overcome, while others may have long-term medical and psychological challenges. Rescues adopting out dogs with long-term medical needs must take great care in selecting the dog's forever family. Sometimes potential adopters want special needs dogs based strictly on emotional reasons; they want to *help* the dogs. This is noble, of course, but *all* potential adopters of special needs dogs should be explicitly informed about the dog's lifetime care and cost. The potential adopter must demonstrate an understanding of the time, energy, and financial considerations these dogs entail before being approved for adoption.

Rescues should regularly evaluate the costs of caring for special needs dogs in order to make more accurate assumptions about financial obligations associated with incoming dogs and to ensure the rescue has the resources to handle them. Regarding adoption fees for dogs with higher lifetime care costs, rescue policies vary. Some reduce the adoption fee for dogs with special needs based on the philosophy that the dog will be expensive for the adopter and a lower adoption fee might make him or her more enticing. Other rescues do not lower their fees for special needs dogs based on the philosophy that a person adopting a special needs dog will have a high lifetime financial burden with that dog and must be committed completely to the dog's care, so they should also be capable of paying the standard adoption fee.

Dogs with special needs deserve to live in happy, loving homes as much as any other dogs. They may be harder to place with forever families, and they may take up more of a rescue's finances, but rescues must remember that for many of these dogs, the rescue is their last chance for *life*. A rescue is truly fulfilling its mission when it is successful in helping the harder-to-place dogs who would otherwise be killed.

Do:

- DO take dogs with special needs into your rescue if they are adoptable. They may take more time to get ready for and to adopt, but they deserve a loving home as much as any dog.

- DO adopt to people who can give the best home to a dog with special needs, ensuring that the applicant is not adopting the dog because he or she "feels bad for him (or her)."

- DO place "special needs" dogs in appropriate foster homes.

Don't:

- DON'T expect a mill dog to know how to behave in a home environment.

- DON'T put a "special needs" dog into a foster home without support and information for the foster family.

- DON'T believe everything stated by a person surrendering a dog; the dog in perfect health may turn out to be a dog with special needs.

- DON'T label a dog as aggressive without having him or her evaluated. He or she may be in pain or just fearful.

- DON'T believe no one will ever adopt one of your rescue's special needs dogs. There's a loving adopter out there for almost every foster dog in your rescue.

Resources:

ASPCA puppy mill information:
http://www.aspca.org/fight-animal-cruelty/puppy-mills/

Best Friends – information about USDA inspections:
http://network.bestfriends.org/9045/news.aspx

Deaf Dog Education Action Fund: http://www.deafdogs.org/

Humane Society puppy mill information website:
http://stoppuppymills.org/

Humane Society puppy mill frequently asked questions: http://www.humanesociety.org/issues/puppy_mills/qa/puppy_mill_FAQs.html

Last Chance for Animals – working to reform pet stores: http://www.milldogrescue.org/

Mill Dog Manifesto: http://upforpups.org/mill-dog-manifesto-ebook/

National Mill Dog Rescue – dog rescue specializing in puppy mill survivors: http://www.milldogrescue.org/

Owners of Blind Dogs: http://www.blinddogs.com/

Pet Store Cruelty – organization raising awareness about pet stores: http://www.petstorecruelty.org/

Puppy Mill Awareness Day – annual events to raise awareness about puppy mills: http://www.awarenessday.org/

Puppy Mill Rescue – nonprofit dog rescue specializing in puppy mill survivors: http://www.puppymillrescue.com/

Puppy Mill Dog's Voice – educational website about puppy mills and pet stores: http://www.puppymilldogsvoice.org/

Prisoners of Greed – puppy mill education: http://www.prisonersofgreed.org/

United Against Puppy Mills – website covering zoning, legislation, and public awareness: http://www.unitedagainstpuppymills.org/

USDA inspections: http://www.aphis.usda.gov/animal_welfare/inspection_list.shtml

Wisconsin puppy mill project – working to end WI puppy mills through education: http://www.nowisconsinpuppymills.com/

Appendix A:
Document Examples

Appendix A is an online supplement to this book available at http://upforpups.org/best-practices-manual/appendices/.

The contents of this appendix have been made available to you by the generosity of the rescuers who assisted in the creation of this manual. Please respect the time and effort they put into developing these documents by using them as learning tools *only*. You are encouraged to study these documents and fashion your own documentation after the concepts represented herein, but using the content of these documents and web pages verbatim is stealing. You wouldn't like it done to you, so please don't do it to others.

Appendix B:
Generic Documents For Your Use

Appendix B is exclusive to purchasers of the paperback *Road to Rescue book.* You may use these documents however you see fit. For your convenience, we have provided these documents online in the Word .doc format at http://upforpups.org/best-practices-manual/appendices/. The password to access this page is "gooddog".

While you will need to alter many areas of these documents to suit your specific needs, the highlighted areas are specific to your rescue and *must* be completed by you before use.

Disclaimer: You *absolutely* should have a lawyer review any legal documents, including the ones herein, before you put them into use.

Contents

- Articles of Organization for a 501(c)3
- Bylaws
- Conflict of Interest policy
- Surrender contract/form
- Intake/evaluation form (should only be used after a dog is evaluated using your rescue's evaluation procedure)
- Volunteer/foster application
- Foster contract
- Foster welcome kit template
- Adoption application
- Adoption contract

About the Author

Kyla Duffy fell in love with dogs after becoming an emergency foster parent for a Boston Terrier with kennel cough. She lives in Boulder, CO with her husband, two rescued kitties (Tux and Chewie), a puppy mill survivor named Bill, and a perpetual stream of foster dogs. She enjoys rehabilitating the tough cases, helping them build up muscle and confidence on long hikes through the beautiful Colorado Front Range.

Kyla is an entrepreneur and athlete, who retired from professional snowboarding in 2001 to pursue more "leisurely" activities, such as adult gymnastics, high-flying trapeze, and aerial fabric. She holds a BS in Marketing, a BA in Spanish Translation, and an MPS in Organizational Leadership. After years of business ownership experience, she founded Happy Tails Books to raise awareness and funding for animal advocacy organizations. She enjoys the creative and philanthropic nature of Happy Tails Books and is always excited to share the passionate stories written by dog-lovers whose animals have clearly changed their lives.

Kyla also founded Up For Pups, a 501(c)3 non-profit organization that serves as a valuable resource for those involved in the animal rescue community. Visit http://upforpups.org find out more about the resources available to you or to book Kyla to come to your area for a presentation about puppy mills, rescue best practices, or "creative volunteerism."